DEEP SOUTH
Discovering My True Sexuality

Jody Dixon

Deep South
Discovering My True Sexuality
Copyright ©2006 by Jody Dixon

All rights reserved. This book may not be reproduced in whole or in part, by any means, electronic or mechanical, without prior written permission from the publisher. For information, or to order additional copies of this book, please contact:

Cypress Hose
155 Cypress Street
Fort Bragg, CA 95437
(800) 773-7782
www.cypresshouse.com

Book design by Brechner & Rosencrans / Cypress House
Cover design by Michael Brechner

    Publisher's Cataloging-in-Publication Data

Dixon, Jody.
  Deep South : discovering my true sexuality / Jody Dixon. -- 1st ed. -- Fort Bragg, CA : Cypress House, 2005.
    p. ; cm.
  ISBN-10: 1-879384-65-5
  ISBN-13: 978-1-879384-65-1
    1. Dixon, Jody. 2. Coming out (Sexual orientation)--Southern States. 3. Gays--Southern States--Identity. 4. Gay men--Southern States--Biography. 5. Southern States--Social life and customs. 6. Southern States--History--Anecdotes. I. Title.
  CT275.D596 A3 2005   2005931155
  975/.0092--dc22 0509

Printed in the United States
9 8 7 6 5 4 3 2 1

*Lovingly dedicated to my parents,
who gave me life and love,
and challenged me to choose
the better part of life*

Introduction

Given that each of us has a unique and highly subjective view of reality, I declare that this is a true story in all its details, save for the names of the people and places described herein. I made these alterations to protect the privacy of my children, my former wife, my sisters, and their families.

The majority of the folks inhabiting this memoir have now, as we used to say, "crossed over," but having grown up in a part of the South where the deeds of grandparents and great-grandparents may be remembered and recounted as vividly as yesterday's trip to the grocery store, I'm taking no chances.

From that disclaimer you might judge me a cautious and sensitive person. True. Yet I will risk the ire of some readers by my very infrequent use of the word "colored" in the historical context of my story to describe an African American or African Americans. I use *colored* only when it seems to be far and away the most appropriate word. I was born in 1930 in a remote rural region of the South where the word "colored"—as in the National Association For the Advancement of Colored People—was the most respectful word one could use for a person of color. I wish to be sensitive to the understandable antipathy many people feel toward descriptors from the era of segregation, but I also want my depiction of those times to ring true.

It may be hard to imagine that the South I was born into less than a century ago could be so little changed from the South of the mid-nineteenth century, but in many respects this was absolutely true. Electricity, telephones, indoor plumbing, paved roads, and countless other modern conveniences we now take for granted were just becoming part of the America where I was born. The rural South of that era was deeply segregated; discrimination against African Americans was endemic and institutionalized. Yet unlike the vast majority of my white peers, and through the unique legacy of my parents and grandparents, I was born and raised in close community with black people, as my story will tell.

Let me hasten to say that this is not a memoir about race relations. The larger story, for which issues of race and class form part of the background, concerns a much more universal drama: sexual evolution in a society that treated any deviation from the most narrowly defined norm as a crime against both humanity and God.

I was sixty-nine years old when I entered intensive therapy. I was beholden to no one regarding that decision. I was no longer married, my children were grown, and my parents were dead. I owed no one an explanation for moving to California and undertaking the most important work of my life: the healing of my fractured psyche. I was determined to answer the question I'd been asking myself since I was twelve: What's wrong with me? I was equally determined to heal my sexual self once and for all.

After two years of intense emotional labor—twenty hours a week of individual and group therapy accompanied by daily journal writing—I emerged from a lifetime of shame into the light of a new life. This book is the story of the family and place I was born to, the childhood and adolescence that formed me, and the guises I assumed throughout my life to mask a truth I once believed to be the worst of sins, and now believe to be divine.

My parents figure largely in this story, and I do not intend to cast them as villains. They were imperfect beings, as we all are. Yet if my story is to be both truthful and helpful, I must

Introduction

reveal some of their imperfect actions. This in no way negates the opportunities and advantages they provided me, which were many, nor does it diminish my admiration for all that they accomplished in their lives. When all is said and done, I am extremely grateful to have been their child.

I believe that each of us is seeking to know and understand what makes us tick, to meet the undisguised self that lives at our core. I further believe that each of us longs to give our genuine self the chance to breathe and speak and dance. Emotional healing involves the clarification of memory; ghostly visions veiled in fear and shame become well-remembered stories about who we really are.

It is my hope that this memoir will trigger your own memories and feelings that may have been obscured by psychic shadows or fearful thoughts about the consequences of revealing your truth. I pray that you will give yourself permission to open fully to whatever emerges from your past. And perhaps you will be emboldened to undertake your own healing journey to liberation from long-suppressed memories and emotions.

DEEP SOUTH

1
When Sonny Shot Ella Mae

I was no stranger to death. Raising animals for food was an integral part of my family's life and I had little emotional attachment to the chickens, pigs, and cattle we routinely slaughtered and ate. By the time I was twelve, I'd shot scores of birds and squirrels with my BB gun. Hunting was one of the only sports I excelled at; I was not the least bit squeamish about bringing down a bird with a good shot. But human death was another matter, and murder was something I'd only heard about until one Saturday night when Sonny shot Ella Mae.

It was a dark and moonless October evening in 1942. The war was on, but it little touched me. I was only twelve and had no older brothers gone to fight. My father was thirty-seven and not inclined to volunteer and leave the enormous responsibility of the farm to anyone else. I was being groomed to one day take over his thousands of acres, his cattle, his fields of cotton and peanuts, his pine woods, and his tenants, white and black—sharecroppers and day help. A nearsighted, sensitive boy on the cusp of puberty, I had no real desire to follow in my father's heroic footsteps, yet I saw no alternative but to do as I was told.

Our family—my mother, father, younger sister Leah, and I—had just returned from our traditional Saturday afternoon trip to Greenville, the seat of Cherokee County on the banks of the Oconee River—the nearest thing to a city in that remote part of Georgia. Work on our farm always stopped at noon on Saturdays; then we and the other white folks who lived on my father's land would get dressed up and drive those thirty-eight miles into Greenville, or fifteen miles on a dirt road to the much smaller town of Cottonwood.

We had gone to a movie matinee in Greenville—Errol Flynn and Bette Davis were big stars of that era—had a quick visit with my favorite cousins, and enjoyed a restaurant supper before heading home at dusk. There was an unspoken imperative that we get back to the home place before darkness fell, because anything might happen on Saturday night. Anything.

Now it was said in those days that the colored folk worked hard during the week and played hard on Saturday night. And it was also said, more crudely, "If you ain't been a nigger on Saturday night, you ain't lived." But for us, the rulers of the farm, Saturday night was a time fraught with the expectation of something bad happening down in the quarter. Those eight simple houses, with their little yards and their narrow porches, were home to upwards of sixty people. On Saturday nights, when bootleg moonshine had done its work, our usually submissive farm hands, many of them the grandchildren of slaves, became restless and argumentative and angry about their terribly hard lives.

When Sonny Shot Ella Mae

I was alone in the living room of that big old house my granddaddy built, warming myself by the fire because with fall finally upon us it was getting chilly in the evenings. I sprawled on the sofa reading the comics in the *Atlanta Journal*, one of the two papers we took to keep us connected to the outside world. My mother was in the sitting room, crocheting another of the hundreds of things that seemed to flow from her fingers like water from a spring. Sister Leah, a beautiful seven-year-old with long brown hair, had gone to bed, and was no doubt speaking seriously to her dolls. My father was out on the front porch, listening to the war news on the radio, the smoke of his cigarette borne through the screen door on a light breeze from the south, the house redolent with the unmistakable scent of his unfiltered Camels.

It was typical of our family to be scattered like that, each of us alone, but all of us in the home, together yet separate. My father was there, yet not there, not really available to me in any deep or intimate way. And my mother, with whom I spent more time than anyone, and who dedicated herself to providing us all we needed to thrive and succeed, was not a friend. There was no one I could share my confusion with. And so, as best I could, I pretended not to be puzzled, and did as I was told. Rebellion was unthinkable. My mother and father were enormously powerful individuals—together they were psychically overwhelming.

My daddy—a handsome man, six feet tall, a trim hundred seventy pounds, and somewhat vain of his appearance—considered himself responsible for everyone who lived and worked on his land. The tenth of twelve children, his parents' favorite son, he was the true heir to his father's moral legacy of ruling with a just and even hand, for which he was well liked and respected by the colored people, and called a "nigger lover" by the envious whites thereabouts. Looking back over the decades, it seems entirely appropriate that Daddy was the one to take over the home place after Granddaddy retired and moved to Greenville.

I finished reading the comics and was about to put another log on the fire and phone my cousin on our brand-new party line, when I heard a young man run up to the house calling, "Mr. Harvey, Mr. Harvey, Sonny done shot Ella Mae."

There it was, that trouble we were forever expecting, though we never spoke of it. In those days, the pervasive racial tension in that part of Georgia was nearly invisible until some eruption in the uneasy peace brought violent rage to the surface. I was not yet conscious of the gross injustice of the society I inhabited, though I knew I was privileged above all black people and many white people, too. And I had known from an early age that the privilege of being the son of Harvey and Clarissa Dixon brought with it every bit as much responsibility as freedom.

My father called to me, "Jody. Come out here."

I could hear in his voice that he wanted to involve me in whatever was going on in the quarter. But why? What could I do about a shooting?

"Yes, Daddy," I said, pushing open the screen door and stepping onto the porch. The young man was at the bottom of the steps, breathing hard, his brow furrowed with worry. I recognized him, of course, though I didn't know his name.

"He says Sonny shot Ella Mae. I want you to go down there and see about it, then come back and tell me what happened."

He nodded slowly to confirm his command; I could tell by the look in his eyes that this was another test for me, another part of preparing me to take over the farm one day, to teach me bravery and responsibility, to be an extension of him. I wonder to this day, sixty years later, if he would have sent me down there on that dark Saturday night had he known the horror that awaited me. I didn't dare ask him to come with me, to reveal how deeply afraid I was.

I got a flashlight from the kitchen, half hoping my mother—small, proud, and full of purpose—would appear and make some protest so I wouldn't have to go. My parents often bickered about what I should or shouldn't be asked to do. Mother wanted me to excel academically, learn to play the piano, and become a cultured person, whereas my father cared little for formal education and looked forward to the day when I would lose my softness and become a man.

But my mother remained in the sitting room, and I had no choice but to follow that frightened young man away from the light of our house and into the darkness. The only light along our way, other than my flashlight, was a single bulb dangling over the porch of the store, a hundred feet from our house.

My heart was in my throat as we hurried past the big barns and the myriad outbuildings barely visible in the gloom that lay between the main house and the quarter. I hated my father for sending me on this onerous errand, yet so great was my desire to please him, to be loved by him, that my hatred was wholly unconscious and would not reveal itself to me for another forty years.

Sonny and Ella Mae's little house—two rooms on the front and two shed rooms on the back—was the first in that line of houses where the day help lived. Ella Mae and Sonny were both in their mid-twenties; they'd been making babies together since their teens; the house was full of children.

There was no electricity in the quarter, and the only light in their house came from the flickering fire in the hearth. I went through the wooden gate of the rusty wire fence that defined their yard and found myself at the back of a mob trying to get inside to see what had happened.

Using every ounce of self-control to overcome my fear, I pushed my way through that crowd of drunk and frightened people, babies crying, children whimpering, the men mostly silent, the women moaning their fears. Then I heard someone say, "Mr. Harvey sent Jody. Get out his way. Let him pass."

As I climbed the three steps onto the crowded porch, I thought I might faint from fear, but I couldn't let anyone know I was afraid. I had to do what Daddy told me to do. I had to see about it and then go back and tell him.

So I took a deep breath, worked my way through the people in the doorway, and turned left into the front room. I practically stepped on Sonny, who was kneeling on the floor, moaning piteously. He was a big man, the best worker among all the day help. He was good-natured, too, except on those nights when he'd follow the creek trail down to where the white trash had their stills, and he'd get some of that wicked moonshine working in him; then he could be a terror, or so I'd heard.

Despite all the people crowded into that little house, there was an open space between Sonny and the fireplace, so I instinctively shined my flashlight on that emptiness and moved the light across the floor to where Ella Mae's body lay. The moaning ceased and every breath was held as my beam illuminated Ella Mae's head—what was left of it—resting against the wall.

Though my every instinct was to see no more and run away, I raised the light above her shattered face and traced the gory trail up to where her exploded brain and fragments of her skull were splattered on the bare wood. Then, as if in a trance, I retraced her slide down the wall and let the light linger on the remnants of her face as I commanded, "Don't leave, Sonny. I'll go get Daddy."

I turned to go and found myself hemmed in by a dozen big men and women, their faces set in agony at the revelation of Ella Mae's death. But nothing could have kept me in that house a minute longer, so great was my fear and revulsion. I pushed past them onto the porch where there were still more people—all the inhabitants of the quarter, drawn by news of the shooting.

When Sonny Shot Ella Mae

I remember thinking that I should say something, for surely Daddy would have said something to reassure them and maintain control, but all I wanted to do was get away as fast as I could and not reveal how terrified I was. As soon as I was out of the light from their fireplace, I took off like a sprinter breaking from the blocks.

I wasn't much of an athlete, and I rarely ran anywhere, but that night I was running so fast from the horror that I felt like I was flying, feet barely touching the ground. I could see our house in the distance, an oasis of light in a world of darkness, and I had no thought but to get there and be safe once more.

As I charged up the slight incline and passed our small dairy barn, I heard my father ask, "Are you okay?"

"Yes," I answered, but I didn't stop running until I reached the house. Then I stood at the bottom of the steps, catching my breath, seeing again the bloody scene, the flickering flames dancing in Sonny's haunted eyes, Ella Mae blown to bits.

Daddy arrived a moment later and said simply, "You're okay."

"Ella Mae's dead," I said numbly. "Sonny blew her brains out."

"Is Sonny still there?"

"Yes," I said, feeling sick to my stomach. "I told him not to leave. I told him I was going to get you."

"Well, I'll call the sheriff," he said, walking up the stairs and disappearing into the house.

And that was that—just another bit of farm business for him to handle. It was as if he had said, "You see, Jody, this is how you do it. This is how a man handles things. No need to get emotional. In fact, emotions just get in the way. And nothing should get in the way of managing the farm. Nothing."

The next morning, I lay in bed exhausted and sad, the scenes of Ella Mae's murder already being stored away in the hidden archives of my brain. I heard the sheriff arrive to pick up Sonny, and I thought Daddy might call me down to tell what I'd seen, but no one called me.

Sonny stood trial, though not before a jury. It was more of a private gathering with the judge, the sheriff, and my Daddy saying, "Now, Sonny Roberts is my very best worker, and I've got to have him for picking the peanuts. And you know it was Saturday night, and they all drinkin'. It's too bad, but I'm sure he didn't mean to do it, and I got to have him for the picking."

Since nobody white got hurt, the judge gave Sonny thirty days in jail; he was only in for three days before Daddy came to get him for the harvest. Slavery may have legally ended in 1863, but people like Sonny and Ella Mae were still little more than slaves, my father their master, and a good one compared to most.

I still sometimes wonder about those little children and what happened to them with their mother gone. They were probably sent to live with a grandmother or an aunt—somebody already overburdened with mere survival. And try as I might, I cannot recall that my father or anyone else ever again mentioned the night Sonny shot Ella Mae.

In therapy, looking back on this most traumatic event, I felt a sharp pang of disappointment about being so thoroughly ignored in the aftermath of my ordeal. I had accomplished an important and difficult task, yet my father never acknowledged what I had done. Intellectually, I understood that he was teaching me how to take care of business and how to comport myself in a crisis, but emotionally, I felt dismissed and devalued, as if my feelings were of no consequence whatsoever.

2
Mother's Kingdom

My memory of the night Sonny killed Ella Mae didn't break through the blockades of my subconscious until I was fifty. My wife and I had just begun therapy for the first time, a process precipitated by our twelve-year-old daughter—one of our five children—having a difficult time communicating with us. She would fall impenetrably silent for long periods of time, and we sought professional help for her. Not long after she began therapy, her psychiatrist suggested that my wife and I also enter individual and group therapy. It was during this therapy that I first recalled the murder of Ella Mae.

Therapy is in large part the mining of memory. By taking me back to significant places and moments in the past, formal therapy challenged me to probe below my surface recollections and confront my *feelings* about the experiences comprising my life.

Raised to be a farmer, I nevertheless became a businessman and a city dweller. This is no great surprise given that my nursery—the place where I spent most of my early childhood—was the store, a big, airy building that stood a stone's throw from the main house. The store was my mother's domain from early morning until dark. When she wasn't tending to customers, keeping books, or stocking and tidying the shelves, she was sitting at her Singer pedal sewing machine making sack-like dresses for the farm women or sewing finer clothes for herself or my sister Leah. Like my father, Mother had boundless energy, and my earliest memories are of being with her in that vast, high-ceilinged room, living out our days in service to the people—black and white—for whom the store was the source of everything needed to sustain them.

Built by my granddaddy in the early 1900s of virgin pine cut and milled on our land, the big white building with its high ceilings, steeply pitched roof, and wood floor, was a true general store. We sold foodstuffs, hardware, fuel oil, gasoline, and myriad farm supplies. Primarily intended to provide for our family and those laborers and sharecroppers residing on our land, our store was also open to the general public. We were the only such store for miles around. It was "fifteen miles to a loaf of bread" on a dirt road to Cottonwood, and thirty-eight miles on pavement to Greenville. In the depths of the Depression, most poor people in the South did not own cars, so our store was literally the economic and social hub of that little corner of the world.

Mother and Daddy even supplied the coffins for our community. In the early days of their marriage, until he became too busy with his other farm work, Daddy built the coffins himself. He was an excellent woodworker; the coffins he made of virgin pine were beautiful. He crafted them as he would a fine cabinet, using dowels instead of nails, and dovetailing the pieces together with pleasing precision. When the corpse in question was a woman, Mother lined the casket in pink sateen; when a man died she lined the casket in blue sateen. In either case, she expertly pleated the edges of the fabric with upholstery tacks. There were three churches on Daddy's land: one for the white sharecroppers, and two for the colored people; each had its own

Mother's Kingdom

graveyard. Though my father and I were officially members of *both* colored congregations—dues five dollars per annum—we attended the Methodist church in Cottonwood.

My mother was the queen of the store and I her only princeling. I was making change from the time I was five and had to stand on tiptoes to see into the cash drawer. I teethed on commerce and learned the cost and value of things long before most children learned their ABCs. While other boys were playing baseball and rough-and-tumble games, I was with my mother in the store. My father was rarely present, being occupied with the larger work of the farm; my longing for him was profound as far back as I can remember. Indeed, some of my very earliest memories are of feigning sleep so that Daddy would be enlisted to carry me.

At the end of a long day—we almost always stayed open until after dark—Mother would take a bolt of cloth and place it on the counter to make my pillow, and there I would fall asleep while she finished up her business. If my father chose to end his workday by coming into the store to help Mother, and I *seemed* to be asleep when they were ready to close, he would pick me up and carry me to the house. So delicious was this physical contact with him, and so rare, that I became adept at pretending to be asleep and keeping up my charade until he had laid me on my bed where my mother would get me into my pajamas. I remember only a few other moments in my life when my father touched me.

Yes, the store was my mother's kingdom, and she thrived on being so essential to so many people. She came from the rural poverty of Tobacco Road in northern Georgia, the middle child of nine. Her father, a subsistence farmer, died before I was born; I remember her mother as lackluster and complaining. My mother was a short, sturdy woman, fastidiously clean and always fashionably dressed, who made of herself a schoolteacher despite the less ambitious tendencies of her parents and most of her siblings. Her marriage to my comparatively wellborn father was a great coup; the story of their meeting and courtship gives a glimpse of how primitive life was in that part of America in the 1920s.

Long before the stock market crash of 1929 brought on the nationwide Great Depression, a severe farming depression had gripped Georgia for many years. My grandfather's resounding success as a farmer in that time and place was an accomplishment of mythic proportions. And my father, ever known as Daddy, would amplify and modernize my grandfather's accomplishments, though not before he left home at fifteen to see the world and return six years later to work for Granddaddy.

At twenty-one, Daddy cut a romantic figure; he was tall and handsome, strong and clever, and worldly, too, having lived and worked in San Diego, Los Angeles, and San Francisco. He drove a red Ford roadster convertible, dressed in style, lived a comfortable life compared to most people in rural Georgia, and was hardworking, honest, adventurous, and proud.

The story goes that shortly after Daddy came back to live with his parents and a few other siblings in the main house, a young schoolteacher rented a room a quarter mile down the road in Lawrence and Ruby's house, Lawrence being one of Daddy's older brothers. The teacher's name was Clarissa Faith Stapleton, and she taught in the one-room schoolhouse—first grade through eighth—about a mile away on the other side of Cypress Creek. That winter there was so much rain that Cypress Creek flooded over the bridge to the school. Daddy, the dashing Good Samaritan, went down every morning with a rowboat and ferried Clarissa across the torrent and brought her back again every afternoon until the creek resumed its normal flow. Hence he was her hero right from the start.

Though they may not have looked a match, they were both

eager to rise in the world, and both were eager to marry and start a family. Granddaddy prodded Daddy to woo Clarissa by promising him the little red house as a starter home, and so my father began dating my mother in earnest. As it happened, she made herself even more desirable by moving back to northern Georgia after only one year as the local schoolmarm; she was lonely for people she knew. So my father pursued her to north Georgia. They married soon after, on Christmas Eve of 1927, and he brought her home to start their life together on the farm they would one day own. My father was twenty-three when they wed, my mother six months younger.

Mother took charge of the store and carried on the traditions of meticulous record keeping, thrift, and honesty established by Granddaddy. I was born on March 21, 1930 in Putney Hospital in Greenville. I was not breastfed, nor was either of my sisters. The custom of the day dictated that anyone who could afford to should feed their children cow's milk from bottles, and so it was that only the children of the poor benefited from all those fabulous antibodies we now know come from mother's milk.

Though my first playmates were black children, I knew from a very early age that our lives might only intersect at the store; they were not to come to my house and I was not to go to theirs. Thinking back on this enforced isolation, I have often wondered if I was lonely as a child. More than loneliness, I remember feeling *different* from other people—white or black—and therefore separate. Long before a more palpable sexual confusion claimed me in my adolescence, I felt myself a stranger in the larger landscape of the farm, the thousands of acres comprising the Dixon place. Even in the store, though I knew everyone and everyone knew me, I stood apart, and not just because I was often behind the counter, but because I was the child of parents who held the reins of power. Without the industry and ambition of my grandfather and father and mother, hundreds of people would have been without work, sustenance, and housing in those extremely hard times.

Whenever serious illness or injury befell one of the tenant women or her children, Mother would visit them every day with soup and comforting words. That a white woman of her status would willingly enter the home of a black person to feed and nurse them earned my mother the reputation of a saint. She shared my father's sense of responsibility for the well-being of all the people who lived on our land, and she reveled in her public persona as a most exemplary Christian.

Working in the store was often fun for me, especially if I liked the person I was waiting on. But there were some customers I wanted nothing to do with and I would attend to them only if Mother was unavailable. One such customer was Hick Johnson, a dirty, smelly old farmer who lived about four miles away and came into the store once a month to buy kerosene and little else. Because Hick was brother to Hugh, who was married to my father's Aunt Vera, he claimed to be our kin and therefore worthy of a discount on his purchases.

He would arrive in his rickety wagon drawn by a horse so malnourished you could see the poor animal's ribs. Hick's mouth was always full of chewing tobacco, the juice dribbling out the corners of his mouth and soaking into his scraggly beard. He would spit big gobs of that vile gunk on the porch and on the floor of the store. Hick seemed to have a preternatural sense of when I would be alone in the store.

He would purchase two gallons of kerosene, which I would draw from the tank at the back of the store, and then he would put a quarter on the counter, though the price was fifteen cents a gallon. When I would ask him for a nickel more, he would say, "But I'm family, you know, and we get two gallons for a quarter."

"I'm sorry," I would say, holding my ground. "It's fifteen cents a gallon."

He would spit on the floor a few more times, tell me for the hundredth time that we were family, and then stuff his mouth with fresh tobacco, scratch himself, and start spitting again. Considering what a disgusting mess Hick made, and all the time it took to clean up after him, I probably should have just given him the discount and been done with it, but I'd been taught by that every penny counted, and a nickel was *five* pennies, so I never let him wear me down.

I have countless memories of the goings-on at the store, but I recall most vividly the approach of sundown when all the farm hands, sharecroppers, land owners—everybody for miles around—would come to buy what they needed for supper. The front porch would be crowded with people gossiping and laughing, drinking coke, smoking Prince Albert tobacco or Camels or Lucky Strike or Chesterfields, and dipping snuff if they were feeling rich. Snuff was a big thing back then, Buttercup the most popular brand among the women. Most of the men chewed tobacco—Brown Mule, Days Work, and Bloodhound—if they didn't smoke, but they might do both.

The front yard, the grass and dirt beneath the oaks and a few longleaf pines, would be full of horses and wagons and beat-up cars and trucks. This was the peaceful mingling of black and white, the poor and the not so poor, young and old. My mother and father were at the heart of this communion, keeping the store open until everyone was served.

Our custom, perhaps begun by Granddaddy, was to lock up the store only after the last person had gone home. And everybody *would* go home when Mother or Daddy simply *closed* the door of the store. It was as if that door were the symbolic gateway to the farm itself; the minute it was shut, people would say their good-byes and leave.

Then a deep silence would descend with the darkness, and we would emerge, lock the door, and walk those hundred feet to home. The light over the porch of the store would stay on all night, blending with the light that hung over the side porch of the main house, illuminating all the ground in between so that we might never be disconnected from the heart of the farm.

3
The Unwanted Nanny

My sister, Leah, was born when I was five. Her arrival changed my status from only child to oldest child, but she came too late to alter the consequences of my deep enmeshment with my mother. I was a quiet boy, my aggressive tendencies muted by Mother's disapproval of any sort of rowdiness. My black hair was always clean and parted neatly, every hair in place. My clothes were always freshly laundered and pressed, and whenever I chanced to get a little dirty, my mother would berate me to take more care. She was obsessed with appearances, especially her own and mine, and she succeeded in transferring that obsession to me. I loved to play with my little metal cars in the sand out under the oak trees, but because the resultant soiled knees and dirty hands always brought on my mother's fussing, I did more and more of my playing on the front porch of the store.

The imminent arrival of a sibling was thrilling for me; when my parents consulted me about a name for the child I was ecstatic. I chose Leah because I thought it such a pretty name; I was very proud to have named her, and I felt quite possessive of her.

Then Aunt Lucille arrived to assume the role of nanny. She was my great-aunt, the sister of my father's mother, and I disliked her from the moment she arrived. Aunt Lucille was not unkind, but rather indifferent to me and not the least bit nurturing. She was fifty-five, had false teeth that clicked and clacked when she spoke, and she wore a hearing aid, the batteries and receiver of which hung around her neck. This device—awful to me—would periodically emit a screeching sound; it seemed Aunt Lucille was forever adjusting the volume and fiddling with the earpiece. She had an odor, too, that came from some soap or cream she used. To my five-year-old nose, she stunk. I would often smell her before I would hear her, for she moved silently about the house and would materialize as if from nowhere, which always made me cringe.

In retrospect, I realize she was just a sad, lonely woman, displaced after years of being a housemother in a Baptist children's home. Widowed young, she had valiantly raised her four children all by herself; she was a family member and needed a job. I'm sure Aunt Lucille was a big help to my mother, but I had no sympathy for her then, knowing nothing of her difficult life. I may also have been unconsciously disdainful of her poverty. My parents were fastidious in their dress and personal habits. Aunt Lucille struck me as slovenly. She dyed her hair dark brown in a futile attempt to cover the gray. I never saw her laugh and I never felt she liked me.

I much preferred Pearl, the sweet black woman who was our cook. She was tiny—less than a hundred pounds—pleasant and gentle and always ready with a smile for me. She never touched me—that kind of intimacy was forbidden between us—but I believe she loved me in her own way, and I certainly considered her an important friend. She was a good country cook, which meant she fried almost everything in pork fat. As far back as I can remember, one of my greatest pleasures was sitting in the kitchen with Pearl, sopping a biscuit with sugar-cane syrup. Or better yet, I'd have a piece of Pearl's incomparable cornbread crumbled in a glass of milk with a tad of salt—heaven!

Pearl came to us early in the morning to prepare breakfast. Then she cooked dinner—the main midday meal—cleaned up the kitchen, and went home at three in the afternoon. The

The Unwanted Nanny

house always felt much friendlier when Pearl was in the kitchen. I wished and prayed she could be Leah's nanny, but I knew she couldn't because she had too many other duties.

Fortunately, my dislike of Aunt Lucille was the exception, not the rule, when it came to my relatives. I loved Mother's youngest brother, Earl, who lived with us for a time and worked for Daddy. I had a red wagon, and sometimes Earl would tie a rope to its long handle, affix the other end to the horn of his saddle, and tow me behind his horse down the sandy road toward Uncle Lawrence's. There were maybe fifteen feet between my wagon and the horse's hooves. Earl would start the horse walking, and then once I was rolling he'd kick it into a canter. I never wanted those rides to end, and I'll never forget how warm and friendly Earl was to me, especially in contrast to Aunt Lucille's coldness.

One Saturday night when my parents were late returning from town, Aunt Lucille said to me, "Jody, we need a bar of soap from the store. Can you run down there and get one for me?"

"Okay," I said. "Do you have a penny?"

She gave me a quizzical look, adjusted her hearing aid, and asked, "Why do you need a penny?"

"Well," I lied, "for every bar of soap I get out of the store for the house, I have to put a penny in the cash drawer."

She made no other comment and gave me a penny.

I was obviously fibbing, but I was only five and thought I'd tricked her. Aunt Lucille knew we never paid for supplies from our store. Nevertheless, when she gave me that penny I felt triumphant. I took the key from the nail by the back door and ran to the store, exultant in my childish belief that getting a penny out of Aunt Lucille was a victory over her.

If that was not the first time I ever unlocked a door, it was nearly the first; I fumbled getting the key in. I pushed opened the door and switched on the inside light—the electricity supplied by our very own Delco system—and gazed around the store half-expecting Mother to be there. I made my way past the wire cage that enclosed the front section of the counter where Mother made out purchase invoices and kept records of farm expenses. People who lived and worked on the farm rarely used cash, their expenditures being subtracted from their pay at the end of the week. Only outsiders paid cash, and it occurs to me now that getting that penny from Aunt Lucille may have been my way of branding her an outsider.

There was still a little warmth coming from the potbellied stove that stood in the center of the room, its tin chimney rising straight up through the twelve-foot-high ceiling into the attic. I scampered past the rounded glass cabinet where we kept a pleasing assortment of candy and other small items—shoelaces and such—that would be easy to steal. I mostly remember the candy: five-cent Baby Ruths, Tom's Peanut Butter Bars for a penny each, and nickel bags of Tom's salted peanuts from our very own central Georgia.

As I came around the end of the counter I felt the coolness from the refrigerated cabinet at the back of the store where we kept the meats, hog headcheese, and other perishables. Then I moved down the aisle between the counter and the shelves that rose tier upon tier to the ceiling along the entire wall. I put Aunt Lucille's penny in the cash drawer and chuckled at having fooled her. Then I climbed up on a little wooden stool, grabbed a bar of Lux, and retraced my steps homeward.

The next morning, Sunday, we had our usual breakfast of pancakes and bacon before putting on our going-to-church finery and driving to Cottonwood, where Daddy and Mother were leading lights of the Methodist church. Daddy was a steward and Mother presided over the preschoolers for Sunday school, so I was with her even then.

When we got home from church, I changed out of my Sunday best and put on my play clothes. At my mother's insistence,

I dressed well even for play: cotton shorts or khaki pants, depending on the weather, a belt, a button-down shirt with a collar (*not* a T-shirt), matching socks, and brown, lace-up rubber-soled shoes.

But before I could leave the house to play, Daddy said he wanted to talk to me in Granddaddy's room, so I followed him through the living room into the bedroom that Granddaddy used whenever he came out from Greenville to visit the farm. Granddaddy still owned 500 acres of the farm at that time, and though Daddy ran the show by then, Granddaddy liked to spend a day at the home place every week, especially when the weather was good.

As I followed Daddy into Granddaddy's room, I knew something unusual was about to happen, since Daddy rarely spoke to me in private. It had never occurred to me that Aunt Lucille would tattle on me, so I was initially more curious than afraid. But when Daddy glowered at me and said, "Aunt Lucille says you took a penny from her for a bar of soap," I knew I was in big trouble. Then he clenched his fists and said, "She says you told her that was a rule, and you know that's a lie."

I watched in disbelief as my father went to the wall where my grandfather kept the double razor strop he used for sharpening his straight razor. For those readers born after razor strops became obsolete, imagine two parallel strips of leather about three inches wide and two feet long. One end would be hooked to the wall so the strop could be pulled taut and a razor blade drawn across its surface to sharpen the steel.

Daddy got this fearsome thing down and let it dangle from his mighty hand. Then he said, "Bend over the bed."

"Don't hurt me, Daddy," I whimpered, terrified.

"Bend over," he growled, his usually calm countenance deformed by a snarl.

Until that moment I had never greatly feared my father. I was in awe of him and hungered for his attention and approval, but he had never hit me even lightly, and his verbal rancor had never been directed against me. Now, suddenly, out of all proportion to the crime, came a furious man with a whip to strike a defenseless little boy. And not just once, but many times.

I present that picture of a little boy attacked by a grown man to help myself comprehend the horror of his assault. I would spend forty-five years trying to suppress my rage at him for his abuse, and to this day I feel a strong compulsion to describe his violence as somehow defensible.

I began to scream before he struck me, and I did not stop screaming until my mother came to the rescue. Before she could arrive, he struck me countless times, the twin straps landing in quick succession on my little buttocks, his fury growing as he beat me, his force increasing with each punishing blow.

The pain was overwhelming—cutting, stinging, stabbing—and God knows how long he would have continued striking me had my mother not rushed into the room shouting with all the force she could muster, "Stop, Harvey. Stop it. That's enough! Stop!"

So Daddy stopped, hung the strop up on the nail, and said breathlessly, "That will teach you not to lie."

Then the larger pain came; my butt was lacerated and blistered and began to swell. And beyond the physical pain was a terrible grief I could not name until a lifetime later when therapy gave me the appropriate vocabulary. My father had violated the boundaries of my being. He had shown himself fully capable—and with little provocation—of killing me. But the greater source of my grief was that I could no longer trust that he loved me.

My father never mentioned the beating and never struck me again. He never had to. I had been subjugated, conquered, and would never knowingly expose myself to such torture again. I would hide my real face behind the mask of a perfectly obedient son.

This is not a recovered memory. I never forgot the beating as I would forget—block—Sonny's murder of Ella Mae. What I did block about the beating, however, was my rage at being so abused for simply being a little boy acting out in a harmless way his displeasure at the presence of an unwanted surrogate mother.

The myth I created to keep my father's image acceptable to me was that he was justified in punishing me for lying. But the truth was that he brutalized me for deviating from the strict personal and social behavior prescribed by my grandfather and carried on by my father. I was the sole male heir to the legacy Daddy wanted to perpetuate. Barring the birth of another, better, son, I was his one hope for the continuance of the farm and our extraordinary way of life.

From the day of the beating onward, I carried the weight of Daddy's expectations on my back. Fearing my father, I became even more emotionally entwined with my mother, who had saved me. She was extremely attentive and nurturing throughout the long healing process. I could not sit down for days, and when at last I could, required a pillow until my wounds were sufficiently healed.

And so, at the age of five, I made it my credo to *never* tell a lie yet my true desires and impulses were thereafter buried under the biggest lie of all—the false self.

4
The Pioneer Patriarch

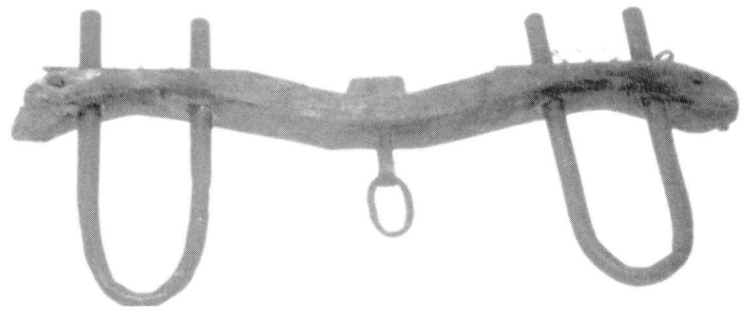

My father was an intelligent man who prided himself on being as modern as one could be in that out-of-the-way part of the world we inhabited. He may have had a brief pang of conscience about how *hard* he beat me, but the beating itself would not have seemed inappropriate to him. "Spare the rod and spoil the child" was still a dominant child-rearing philosophy in those days, and beatings had been an integral part of my father's upbringing. Twenty-five years separated us, but the world he was born into was far more physically demanding than the easy one he worked so hard to make for me.

A novelist could not invent a more symbolically appropriate site for my beating than my grandfather's room. Daddy's use of Granddaddy's razor strop to punish me only adds to the mythological perfection of the story. That room represented my grandfather's persistent presence in our lives, and I believe it was Granddaddy's spirit that lifted his son's hand against me.

The Pioneer Patriarch

My grandfather, known to everyone outside our family as Mister Edward, was a stern, conservative Methodist who believed the Bible to be the literal truth and white men superior to all others. He was incredibly hardworking and frugal, and nearly every endeavor in his life proved profitable. He began with nothing and finished with a large fortune. He established the place and form for my father's life, hence for mine. Deception and dishonesty were not part of that form, which is why my father reacted so swiftly and ferociously to my childish fraud. By modern psychological standards my father's beating me was inexcusable, but given our family history, his actions make a certain tragic sense.

Granddaddy—Edward Henley Dixon—was born in 1860 just as the Civil War began. He was five years old when it ended, and he grew into manhood as the South lay in ruins. He was born in Bush County, one of the most sparsely populated and backward parts of Georgia, the ratio of black people to white more than seven to one.

When he was twenty, Granddaddy borrowed money at usurious rates to buy fifty acres of relatively level ground fifteen miles from the hamlet of Cottonwood and forty miles from the larger town of Greenville. His land was forested with virgin longleaf pine, the topsoil sandy loam.

He built a one-room log cabin, where he lived with his mother. Working alone from dawn until dusk, using an ax, a saw, and oxen to pull the stumps and clear the timber, he plowed that precious soil, planted his crop of cotton, and within two years made enough money to pay off the loan. This was a remarkable accomplishment.

His mother died when Granddaddy was twenty-three. As the story was told to me, he grew lonely, and one evening after a long day of toil he rode his mule two miles to the McAllister family farm and told Mary, who was fifteen, that he wanted to come courting her. Mary allowed that he could, but said that in future he must bathe and put on clean clothes before coming to see her. He promised he would. They married shortly thereafter and remained devoted to each other for sixty-seven years, her death following his by a matter of months. They had twelve children—only one died in infancy—and together they experienced the advent of electricity, automobiles, airplanes, telephones, radios, nuclear bombs, and indoor plumbing.

Building on his initial success, and with his quiet, steady helpmeet keeping him well fed, Granddaddy began buying up the surrounding land and employing colored day help to build his empire. When he "retired" at the age of seventy he had accumulated 2500 acres. He then gave each of his ten surviving children two hundred acres, while retaining five hundred and that one room in the home place for his weekly visits.

I put quotation marks around *retired* because Granddaddy barely slowed down after moving into the beautiful new house he built in Greenville. Shortly after settling down in that more urban place, he built twenty duplexes and rented them out. Then he set up an office at the back of his house and went into the money-lending business. When he died at age ninety-one, Granddaddy left some $300,000 —a huge sum in 1951—duplexes, several houses, and land. Before I tell the story of the reading of his will, I want to describe his first great house—known ever after as the home place—and the farm infrastructure he created.

The big two-story house where I spent my childhood was built in 1891 from virgin timber cut and milled on the land. A brother-in-law, aptly named Edwin Carpenter, was the expert builder who presided over the construction, which took place a stone's throw from Granddaddy's original log cabin. Granddaddy's brother, Semi, assisted Edwin in the work. When the big house was completed, the cabin was replaced by a smokehouse.

The home place was the first house in Bush County to have glass windows, and they were big windows, too. It was also the first house in the county to have electricity, which came from the little Delco plant Granddaddy built. In these and many other ways, he was a pioneer of modernity, unafraid to experiment with the latest technological wonders.

Spacious porches girdled the house, which had three big bedrooms and a living room downstairs, the ceilings fourteen feet high. Upstairs was composed of two even larger rooms, their ceilings ten feet high. The boys slept upstairs, the girls and Granddaddy and Grandmother down. Like many homes built in rural areas of the South before electricity and gas became commonplace, the downstairs rooms opened off a central hallway and each had its own fireplace. These four rooms formed a square at the front of the house, behind which stood the dining room, and beyond that, connected to the main house by a porch, was the kitchen. Because its wood-burning stove was the most likely cause of fires, placing the kitchen apart from the rest of the house greatly increased the odds of saving the house in the event of a fire.

What a bustling scene it must have been in the days of Daddy's childhood, Granddaddy up before dawn to ring the big bell that woke his sons for another day of toil. That bell, by the way, hung just outside an upstairs window and must have been painfully loud to those boys sleeping close by.

Upon completion of the main house, Granddaddy built a huge mule barn—mules being the engines of plowing and hauling—a simple sawmill, a blacksmith's shop, a cotton gin, a cane mill, the store, and the houses where the day help lived. They too awoke when the bell sounded, knowing that Mister Edward expected a long day's hard work if they wanted to retain their places on the best farm in the region. Farmers and sharecroppers came from miles around to pay for the use of the cotton gin and the sawmill and to buy supplies from the store.

Along with his cotton crop, Granddaddy planted a highly profitable sixty-acre pecan grove and several acres of sugarcane from which syrup was made for home consumption and sale to stores in the surrounding towns. My father learned to drive a truck when he was eight years old; by the time he was ten he was driving forty miles on a dirt road to Greenville to sell E.H. Dixon cane syrup to scores of eager customers. Allowing a ten-year-old to drive a truck and work a trade is not only illegal now, it would be considered irrational. Yet my father loved both the experience and the responsibility, and it prepared him for the adventure of his lifetime.

My paternal grandmother was a quiet, gentle person who inspired the planting of live oaks around the house that grew into splendid giants. A lover of books, she created a home library, which she called the Oaks Library, that was as good as most public ones of the day. She left the rearing of the boys largely to Granddaddy, while he left the girls to her. There were five boys and six girls, born with clockwork regularity two years apart. The age range was so extensive that my father and some of the younger children had their first years of schooling at home with the eldest sister, Florine, as their teacher.

At some point, Granddaddy built a house in Cottonwood where Grandmother and the school-aged children lived during the week, while he lived at the home place and ran the farm. This served to give Grandmother a bit more of a social life. It's no surprise that none of the boys showed much interest or promise in school, whereas the girls all thrived there. The children who continued to go to school after the eighth grade—my father not among them—were sent to Methodist boarding schools. It was only the girls who went to college; though not all of them graduated, each got a taste of higher education and the loftier realms of culture.

Granddaddy's priorities underscore the origin of my father's personality and ambition, but there was an essential difference between my father and his father. My grandfather was narrow-minded and a racist; Daddy was not. This difference was dramatically revealed when Granddaddy died. His ten surviving children gathered in his big bedroom in Greenville to hear an attorney read the will. When it was announced that Granddaddy had disowned Leon, Daddy's favorite brother, for marrying a half-Indian woman—a divorcee with a child—my father rose and said, "I can't go along with that. I will sign whatever documents are necessary so Leon can have my share." And then he left the room.

That share would have amounted to a great deal of money and property, but Daddy wanted nothing to do with an inheritance tainted by his father's prejudice. The other siblings were moved to agree with Daddy, and the pie was divided ten ways instead of nine. Though it was not Granddaddy's dying wish that Leon receive a dime, I believe he would have been proud of my father, for his devotion to fairness.

My own relationship to Granddaddy and Grandmother was friendly, though they were never physically affectionate with me. I was not afraid of Granddaddy as some of my relatives were. Throughout my childhood, he came to the farm once a week. I admired and respected him, but he was essentially legendary to me; his creation of the farm—carving the fields out of wilderness and building the home place—was the founding myth of our family. When I would visit my grandparents at their home in Greenville, the constant stream of people coming to borrow money from Granddaddy and to ask his advice only added to his godlike stature in my mind. Not a typical old person, he was the patriarch of the Dixon clan, and he set the standard for working hard and making money until his dying day.

5
Mules and Yellow Jackets

One of the most difficult parts of my therapy involved knocking my father off the pedestal I'd kept him on for most of my life. He was a good man in many ways, a great success in his outer life, but he was not comfortable with emotional intimacy, which was a great loss for me. For my mother, Daddy's unwillingness or inability to be intimate with her created an emotional hunger she tried to satisfy through me. To further complicate my emotional puzzle, I was the designated go-between for much of my parents' interaction from the time I was a little boy until I left home for college. I'll say more about that later; this chapter and the next belong to my father.

One poignant memory that emerged in therapy, along with a torrent of tears, was of a recurring drama staged on the porch of the store when I was five and six. Daddy rode a big, beautiful quarter horse named Billy. A graceful, bright-eyed bay with a blaze face, Billy was absolutely loyal to Daddy and would permit no other rider. Daddy spent many hours a day in the saddle, and I envied his relationship with Billy.

Nearly every day, unless he was away on business, Daddy would join us for the midday meal, which we called dinner. He would ride in from the fields or wherever he had been overseeing work, tie up Billy at the store, and walk up to the house. Sam Nelson, who was both a field hand and one of the colored people my father trusted to do more personal chores, like shining his shoes, would always be there to lead Billy to his stall. While Daddy dined, Sam would remove Billy's bridle, give him food and water, wipe him down and brush him, and then bring him back to the store rested and ready for my father's afternoon work.

The memory that arose some sixty-five years after the fact was of little Jody standing on the corner of the porch, holding out his arms and pleading with Daddy, "Take me. Take me. Take me with you."

Daddy would swing into the saddle and reply à la Gary Cooper, "Stay with your mother."

I remember thinking, *Why can't I ride with you? Billy can carry both of us.* But I never dared speak those thoughts aloud. I had known from infancy that my father's word was law. This was his ultimate power over me that would shape the course of my life.

Another early interaction with my father captures the intensity of my unrequited love for him. I was eight years old. It was a hot, muggy Sunday afternoon in summer. Daddy and I came out on the porch after dinner and saw about twenty of our mules a half mile away, sauntering along the county road toward the paved highway. Somebody had forgotten to latch the gate of the corral. Being curious animals, the mules had nosed it open and wandered out for a Sunday excursion. Daddy said, "Come on, let's go," and we hurried to his truck to drive after them.

The mule barn with its large corral was some three hundred yards from the house. We had fifty mules, which meant that fewer than half of them had escaped. Most of the plowing and hauling on our farm was still mule-driven in the late 1930s, so our mules were extremely valuable to us. They were also very big animals, and not worldly-wise, so it was crucial to head them off before they got to the highway.

I felt particularly happy that Daddy had brought me along on this adventure rather than summoning a field hand to help him. He was taking me with him into his world and trusting me, which I found exhilarating. He drove very slowly as we approached the mules, not wanting to spook them. As we drew close, Daddy rolled down his window and spoke gently, calling their names as we edged past them on the dirt road. "Hey Nat, hey Tom. Hey Ethel, hey Mary. Where do you think you're going?"

When we got ahead of the mules, Daddy turned the truck around to face them, then parked. We hopped out and started walking toward them, holding our arms wide and calling out, "Go on, Sam, go on, Pete. Go home." Daddy walked along one edge of the dirt road and I walked along the other, both of us keeping up our friendly chatter. "Go on, Tom, go on, Betty. Get on home." The mules barely hesitated before turning around and heading back toward their barn. They knew who was boss.

That might have been the end of the story, but for the three-foot length of peanut pole I found stuck in the ground on the roadside. What is a peanut pole? Imagine a pole about eight feet long and three inches in diameter made from the trunk of a young pine tree. Standing upright with its point buried in the ground, the pole was perfect for stacking peanut vines. Commonly called *goobers*, peanuts were fast replacing cotton as the main crop in that part of Georgia; Daddy grew hundreds of acres of them. Before automated harvesting took over, the vines were first plowed to clip their tap roots, after which field hands would pull the vines out of the ground, shake off the sandy loam, and stack the vines on the poles. When the stack of vines reached nearly to its top, the laden pole was ready for transport.

How this fragment of a peanut pole came to be stuck in the roadside earth remains a mystery, but I know I wanted it to add authority to my herding. To my surprise, that pole had become a plug in the mouth of a yellow-jacket nest. When I yanked the pole out of the ground, a horde of angry wasps swarmed into the air and the chase was on.

Daddy grabbed me by the hand and we sprinted toward the house as the yellow jackets stung our arms and faces and landed in our hair and stung our heads and crawled down our necks to sting our backs and chests. Anywhere they could get, they got. We charged right through the mules, Daddy pulling me along with such strength that my feet barely touched the ground. When we got to the house, Daddy yelled, "Clarissa! Clarissa!" and we dashed up the steps to the kitchen. My mother rushed to help, stripping me as she killed the yellow jackets still tangled in my hair and under my clothes.

The treatment they used to neutralize that wasp venom was miraculously effective. Daddy ripped open cigarettes and mixed the tobacco with water to make poultices to be pressed onto each bite. I remember he lay on the kitchen floor treating himself while my mother tended to me. We had dozens of bites all over us—the pain was fantastic—but the tobacco poultices quickly drew out the poison and the danger soon passed.

Despite the high drama of the chase and the cure, what remains most vivid for me after all these years was the thrill of my father taking my hand and running with me—pulling me to safety. In the privacy of my thoughts I was overjoyed to have suffered with him, because through our suffering together I had experienced what I longed for more than anything: the strength and security and *proof* of his love

6
Daddy the Adventurer

Who was this father I loved and feared so intensely? And why did I feel so lacking next to him? First of all, every child considers his or her parents all-powerful in the beginning, for they hold our very lives in their hands. In the course of growing up, our parents become more human to us. In the healthy evolution of our psyches we come to see ourselves as their equals. But I was both intimidated by my father and denied emotional and physical access to him, so my only recourse was to either reject him or idealize him, and I chose the latter.

The second part of the answer is that my father's life was easy to romanticize for a boy with my fertile imagination. He left home when he was fifteen years old, surviving on his wits and hard work for six years before returning to Georgia to step into the traces of his own formidable father. Indeed, the favorite stories of my childhood were Daddy's spellbinding accounts of his arduous childhood and his magical journey to California and back.

There is a deeper part to the answer, less understandable to me until decades later, which was that I was in love with *what* he was: a big, handsome man, easy in his body, good with his hands, and instinctively, effortlessly charming.

Even as young boys, my father and his brothers were expected to toil as farm hands to earn their keep. They were forced by circumstances to step out of childhood as soon as they possibly could, and perform as men or suffer the consequences. This no doubt explains why all six of Granddaddy's sons left school early and left home shortly thereafter.

One painfully sad story my father told was of a day when he was eleven years old and planting sweet potatoes with his brother Leon. They became distracted and got to playing some sort of game. With absolutely no warning, Granddaddy rode up on his horse and laid into them with his four-plait whip, striking their backs and arms before riding away without saying a word, his message clear: *We do not play here. We work. If you don't work, you'll be punished.*

So it comes as no surprise that my father left home as a young teen to experience life free of such harsh constraint. Though my own childhood was infinitely less physically demanding than my father's, I too would suffer the constrictions of my father's expectations of how I should behave and what I should become.

Being a competent hand with all manner of farm work, learning to drive at age eight, and being thrust into the role of salesman at ten, Daddy developed valuable skills that would aid him greatly during the grand odyssey he undertook as a boy and returned from as a man.

Tall for his age at fifteen, handsome and self-confident, Daddy went to Jacksonville, Florida, with fifteen dollars. He used the money to enroll in a barber school, and took a part-time job to cover his room and board. He earned his certificate and went to work cutting hair. Bored to tears after a few weeks of barbershop life, Daddy quit just as he was about to be sacked.

Restless, he returned to the home place and worked for Granddaddy at day wages. With World War I still raging, Granddaddy decided it was improper that none of his sons had gone to fight. So he summoned all his male heirs and declared that the family needed to be represented directly in the war effort; he left it to them to decide who should volunteer. Too young to go, Daddy was not a candidate. Frederick, the eldest son, volunteered to volunteer, but before he could sign up, the war suddenly ended.

Daddy worked for Granddaddy until he amassed enough money to give him a good start, and then he set off for California. The year was 1921, California the Promised Land. Daddy hitchhiked through Texas and Oklahoma, finding plenty of work along his way. Ranching was king from Oklahoma westward, and Daddy soon discovered that he greatly preferred ranching to farming. This preference would ultimately result in his pioneering cattle ranching in our part of Georgia.

When he finally arrived in San Diego after a year's travel, Daddy went to work for a man with a large herd of goats. His job was to milk the goats and then deliver the milk, which gave him an opportunity to learn the lay of the land. His knowledge of the area helped him get his next job as a pickup and delivery man for a laundry service. He was so well liked by his employer there that, fifty years later, a Mr. MacDowell arrived at the home place in search of his "good friend" Harvey Dixon.

From San Diego, Daddy moved north to Los Angeles where he had a number of jobs, his favorite being a prop man at the Coconut Grove nightclub. There he met famous singers, celebrities, and movie stars including Rudolph Valentino and the young Joan Crawford. He said the job required him to work long and hard every day but he loved being close to all that glamour.

Then it was on to San Francisco where he got a job in an import-export business. He adored San Francisco and truly left his heart there. Promoted to a managerial position, he wrote home to tell Granddaddy and Grandmother of his success. Granddaddy sent a postcard in reply. It was the only communication Daddy received from home during the entire six years he was gone, though he wrote to his parents every month to let them know he was alive and well. Here is what that postcard said—a succinct elucidation of the Dixon creed.

Son,
It's not what you make,
it's how much you save.
Papa

My parents were married a year after Daddy's return to Georgia. They took up residence in the little red house and worked for Granddaddy during the last few years of his tenure on the land. Upon my grandfather's retirement, Daddy was given 200 acres as well as the responsibility for overseeing the 500 acres Granddaddy still owned. Over the next twenty years, Daddy would buy back the 200 acres given to each of his siblings—with the exception of brother Lawrence's 200 acres—all the acreage comprising Granddaddy's 2500-acre farm, and would ultimately expand his total to 5600 acres. Not long after my sister Dana was born, he renamed the land Joleda Farm for his three children: Jody, Leah, and Dana.

Daddy the Adventurer

Daddy eventually made a national name for himself by introducing large-scale cattle ranching to a part of Georgia where such an undertaking had previously been thought impossible. His herd of registered Herefords would become the largest in the entire Southeast. He ascended to the vice presidency of the American Hereford Association; offered the presidency, he declined because that position required a great deal of public speaking, something he dreaded.

As his father had done before him, Daddy combined relentless hard work with extraordinary foresight and a genius for directing both skilled and unskilled laborers to achieve his lofty goals. He had an ambitious partner in my mother—there was a keen, unspoken competition between them—and there was absolutely nothing more important to him than the farm and its perpetuation. As his only son, seldom a day went by without my being reminded in one way or another that my destiny was to be a direct extension of his.

7
The Go-between

For all my life—and through most of my first year of therapy in California—I encountered a gap in my memory of being seven years old. I began school at six, and have always had clear memories of that important passage, and I remembered many experiences from when I was eight and nine, but Jody at seven was at best a blur.

Whenever I strained my brain in therapy to remember anything about that blurry time, the best I could do was conjure vague impressions of being alone with my mother, but not in the usual way we were so often alone together in the store. There was a claustrophobic feeling attached to these fragments of memory—a sense of being smothered—yet no distinct pictures.

The question "What's wrong with me?" began to plague me at the onset of puberty, when I first sensed that my desires were not quite similar to those of other boys. But another mystery preceded that question by several years, and expressed itself in my mind as "Something is not right about Mother." There was something about her that puzzled and disturbed me: something in her too long, too intimate embraces of me, something in the way she sought to control my behavior and appearance, and something in her eyes when I would look up to find her watching my every move.

That gap in my memory, combined with the suspicion that something had been amiss with Mother, prompted me to undergo hypnosis and visit psychics in hopes of gaining entrance to that forgotten time. I felt close to unraveling the mystery on several occasions, but I entered intensive therapy at the age of sixty-nine still separated from the deeper truth.

I recounted to my therapist my role as the carrier of messages between my parents, and how it wasn't until I left home for college that I realized how emotionally exhausting it had been for me to be their go-between. In retrospect, their means of communicating with each other seems extremely neurotic, but since I'd been born into my role, I had no way of knowing how absurd and damaging the process was for me.

Imagine my mother on a summer evening, crocheting at the kitchen table. My father is out on the porch, not twenty feet away. She calls to me and I drop whatever I'm doing and rush to serve her. "Jody," she says, looking me over with her ever-critical eye to make sure my clothes are clean and my hair in place, "tell your Daddy I'm going into town in the morning and does he need anything."

By *anything* she meant anything for the farm—something from the hardware store or the tractor shop. She could easily have spoken directly to my father, who could hear every word she said to me, but instead she made her speech to me. I would then dutifully carry her message to Daddy and repeat it verbatim; he would give me his answer, and I would come inside and repeat it to my mother.

This bizarre sort of interaction was common when my parents were in the house together. Whatever my mother wished to say to my father, she said through me. They spoke directly to each other only if my father initiated the conversation, and in many of those instances he was caustic or critical, which would usually incite my mother to say, "You don't love me. After all I've done for you, you treat me like this." And then, with a dramatic flourish, she would leave the room, crying.

To make matters stranger still, and to add to my sense that something wasn't right about Mother, she would use that identical "You-don't-love-me" routine with me whenever I did or said something to displease her. She would use the same accusations and the same hyper-emotionality she used with Daddy, which even to my unsophisticated young mind seemed strange and inappropriate.

When I was in the third grade, I brought home a report card on which I'd gotten a C for deportment because I talked out of turn and wrote notes and passed them to my friends. Mother acted as if I'd been convicted of a felony. She launched into her litany of, "How could you do this to me? Is this how you show your love for me? After all I've done for you."

Daddy happened to be home, and rather than follow his usual course of staying out of matters between Mother and me, he came into the kitchen and asked what was going on. Mother held the report card out to him and said, "Look at the grade he got in deportment. I'm so ashamed. His teacher says he talks out of turn and talks to his friends in class, and…"

Daddy took the report card, studied it for a moment and said, "But all the other grades are A's. I say if he can talk and still make A's, let him talk."

This event stands out in my memory because it was so unusual for him to stand up for me against my mother. She, of course, left the room in tears, and it was Daddy who had to sign that report card.

My parents' union and our family life in general was imbued with perpetual tension that caused us all to seek relief by going off into our separate worlds whenever we could. My father left the house early in the morning, returned for the midday meal, and then was gone again until dark. At the end of the day, he kept mostly to himself until bedtime.

Mother worked in the store all day unless she was driving

The Go-between

her children to and from school, and she taught Sunday school, played an active role in church groups, and was always bringing food to people who were ill. And I, not Daddy, was her confidant. I listened dutifully to her gossip and opinions and how her day had gone. I didn't have the option of riding away on a horse.

Early in my marriage, when I was in the army and stationed at Fort Jackson in South Carolina, my wife and I would drive down to the home place for weekend visits. One Sunday, driving back to the base, my wife said, "Jody, are you aware that your family never gathers together and has a conversation except at mealtimes? You'll visit your mother in one room, then get up and go into another room to visit with your father. It's that way every time we come down here."

I thought about it for a moment and said, "Doesn't every family do that?"

"I hope not," she said. "I hope ours won't do that."

Thankfully, my wife and I did not interact in that fragmented way. We made a point of being on the same page as much as possible regarding how we raised our children, and made every effort to keep any difficulties we had with each other separate from our interactions with them.

8
The School Sissy

Children, by Nature's design, are incredibly resilient. My childhood was fascinating and full of drama and good times, too.

Starting school was a great liberation for me. My mother expected me to be a model student, which I attempted to be, but I was far more interested in the social aspects of school. I had been so isolated for the first six years of my childhood that my desire to make friends was intense. My only regular contact with other white children had been at church on Sunday, while my interactions with colored children were limited by the social realities I was born to. Once I started school, I had lots of playmates, both girls and boys, and parties and overnights became a favorite pastime.

The most memorable slumber party I ever gave at the home place was in the fifth grade. The boys all slept in my new bedroom, which Daddy had just added to the house, while all the girls shared another room down the hall. Already possessed of a flair for the dramatic, I got it into my head to pretend to sleepwalk. I waited until I thought everyone was asleep; then I rose, made sure not to step on anybody, and tiptoed out into the hallway. I held my hands out in front of me and made a low moaning sound as I shuffled along. My friends began to whisper to each other, and shortly thereafter all the kids were awake and watching me. When their talk got loud enough, I opened my eyes and feigned surprise to find myself away from my bed. I'm certain most of them believed I was sleepwalking.

The School Sissy

At another such party, some of the boys caught a whole bunch of little green tree frogs and let them loose in the living room, causing a general riot among the girls. Daddy, who generally left our oversight to Mother, appeared in the living-room doorway and ordered the house cleared of frogs. I did not instigate the frog incident. For one thing, I would never have defied my parents in such a way; for another, I wasn't much interested in the usual shenanigans of boys.

Indeed, my introduction to sports at school—a softball game at recess—made it clear to me that heroics on the playing field were not to be part of my destiny. I came to bat, struck out, and then, as I was returning to the sidelines, someone shouted, "Jody, you hold a bat like a girl." I didn't pick up a bat again for forty-eight years. I want to share the story of that next at bat because it illuminates how deeply the fear of being thought effeminate affected me.

The youth group at our church in Lexington scheduled a father-son softball game at a city park. My youngest son asked me to play with him and I felt obliged to agree. During the weeks leading up to that game, my stomach was in knots. I was visualizing myself standing at the plate, determined to hit the ball. When that dreaded moment arrived, I strode to the plate and smacked the first pitch to center field. With everybody cheering me on, I sprinted to first base. When the center fielder bobbled the ball, I took off for second. When his throw sailed over the infield, I kept going to third, and when the throw from the catcher went between the legs of the third baseman and into left field, I scurried home—a home run! My son, who knew nothing of my past trauma, congratulated me with a "Way to go, Dad!" and I was tearfully relieved to be a momentary hero instead of a loser. I went to bat twice more and struck out both times, but no one seemed to notice because I had opened my show with that home run, however improbable.

Every morning during the school year, Mother drove me fifteen miles to Cottonwood Elementary, then drove home to open the store. Every afternoon she'd make the same thirty-mile round trip to pick me up and bring me home. Though there was bus service to an elementary school in Bush County only three miles from our house, Mother was determined that my sisters and I attend the much better school in Cottonwood. Since our farmland was in both Bush *and* Mitchell counties, we were given permission to attend Cottonwood Elementary. My mother drove those sixty miles every day so we would get the best education possible—an act of devotion for which I will be forever grateful.

Cottonwood Elementary was a large one-story building of red brick, its front porch featuring a four-column Colonial façade. I attended grades one through seven there, with about fifteen kids to a class. I enjoyed school, for the most part, though recess time was a source of anguish because I felt so inept as an athlete. Whenever possible, especially if a ball game was going on, I stayed in the classroom and did my homework or worked on special projects for extra credit. I also frequently complained that my legs ached. When my mother took me to a doctor to investigate my claims, the doctor suggested, "Jody has growing pains." This did little to lessen my fear of being thought of as the school sissy, but it gave some credence to my not going out much at recess. I loved rainy days because we all had to stay inside, and my excuses were unnecessary.

There was no lunchroom at school and most of the kids brought sack lunches. But Mother arranged for Miss Nell—a close friend in Cottonwood with her own children my age—to provide me a hot lunch. Every day at noon I would walk the mile to Miss Nell's house, enjoy a scrumptious hot meal, and then walk back to school. She charged my mother twenty-five cents a day. I ate like a king, and I especially remember her fried cornbread.

The School Sissy

Speaking of twenty-five cents, that's how much the Monday matinee cost at the Cottonwood Theater, plus five cents for popcorn. Since my mother had a meeting of her Ladies' Circle at the Cottonwood Methodist church every Monday afternoon at three, I would usually walk from school to the movies, where Mother would pick me up after the show. On other days, when she had errands to run in town, she would drop me off at a classmate's house to goof around for an hour or so until she came to get me. Goofing around meant playing hide-and-seek, hanging around the courthouse square, or walking down to Cypress Creek.

Upon our return to the farm in the afternoon, we would reopen the store, where I would do any homework I had and then either help in the store or play until dark. Sometimes I'd ride my bicycle, though there were no paved surfaces on the farm. It wasn't easy riding on dirt, but I enjoyed it. My father helped me learn to ride, and that was special for me. I got the bike for Christmas when I was eight; that being the Christmas I concluded there was no Santa Claus because I couldn't imagine how anybody could have gotten my bike down the chimney.

Mother was eager to give me any available educational advantage. Along with my regular schooling, she signed me up for extra classes with Miss Dola, who would later become my piano teacher. Miss Dola taught a class called "Reading," which was really memorization. We learned all sorts of topical rhyming poems and stories, one of which I performed at an assembly in front of the entire elementary school when I was eight years old.

What makes this recital particularly fascinating to me, looking back on it, was that I performed the piece in blackface, which was not at all unusual in that era, and my performance was greeted with the loud applause I was by then accustomed to inspiring. The purpose of the poem—in the context of an all-white school in one of the most segregated societies in

America—was to humanize black people, yet maintain the prevalent stereotypes and class divisions. The poem differentiates between "good" white people and "white trash." Here is the text of the poem, complete with its intentionally bad spelling to simulate the vernacular.

His Viewpoint
There's lots of white boys living
In de alley back of us
An' when I was out dere playing
Dey sho' did raise a fuss
Callin' me a lil' nigger what de
Lawd done made at nite,
An' when I run in to Mammy,
Dey tripped me up for spite.
What do you reckon dat she said
After she got thru cuddlin' an'
Pattin' me on my head —
She said, "Sammy honey, you is yore
Ole mammy's mash,
Don't you mind dim common chillun,
Dey ain't nuthin' but ole white trash."
So now I declare I don't mind nuthin'
I pass dem white boys with a dash
I'd ruther be a high-toned nigger
Dan ole' pore white trash.

I got my first pair of glasses the year I turned nine. I was the only boy in school who wore glasses. The *only* one! As if that weren't traumatic enough for a boy in those days when very few boys wore glasses, my mother decided I should also start taking piano lessons—*at school!* I pleaded with her to spare me that humiliation, but she thought the advantages would outweigh the accompanying ridicule, and so I became the only boy in our school to take piano lessons from Miss Dola.

The dreaded piano room was on the second floor just off the playground, and as I trudged up those outside stairs, I imagined every boy in the school watching me, which made every step feel like a mile. I took lessons for a scant nine months, an ongoing nightmare for me, though I loved music. When I was in high school and singing in the choir, I regretted not having learned to play the piano, but taking lessons in elementary school was a terribly stressful experience.

In therapy I realized that no one ever actually called me a sissy. Indeed, I know that I was accepted and liked by all the boys my age. Yet I *felt* like a sissy, which only amplified my sense of separation from my male peers and added to my feelings of emotional isolation. I *did* do all the things that only girls did: I wore glasses, took piano lessons, held a bat the wrong way, and abhorred roughhousing and games involving physical contact. I never learned to play ball games, never wrestled or fought. Yet I was ambitious, energetic, and extremely sociable, so I naturally sought other ways to excel.

As I grew older and more opportunities presented themselves, I took up public speaking, acting, singing, and dancing, all of which gave me ways to be recognized as exceptional. Thank God there was no shame attached to participating in those kinds of extracurricular activities. Performing allowed me to express my inherently outgoing nature. Yet for all my success, my sense of being effeminate and my fear of being perceived as girlish would haunt me for many years to come.

I will end this chapter with a recollection of my first kiss, which I distinctly remember, and which Betty, the heroine of this brief romance, claims to have no memory of. Several decades have intervened, but I can still feel her breath on my ear as we hid under the table in the school library—we were in the third grade—whispering to each other. I was suddenly overcome with an urge to kiss her. I closed my eyes and pressed my lips to her cheek. Shocked and dismayed by my show of affection, she crawled out from under the table and hurried away. I stayed put awhile longer, puzzled and disappointed at her not returning the favor.

9
Cousin Johnny

Some of the fondest memories of my preadolescent years are of the twice-yearly family reunions held at the home place. We would gather for big, informal feasts—Granddaddy and Grandmother, Daddy and Mother, and all my aunts and uncles and cousins—at Thanksgiving or Christmas and the Fourth of July. Granddaddy and Grandmother may have been the hereditary heads of the clan, but Mother and Daddy were decidedly the center of family gravity at these reunions.

I loved all my cousins and was always excited to see them. They were my surrogate siblings, in whose midst I felt relieved of the incessant pressure to be the most exemplary of children. I was part of a gang when the cousins came, and there was a certain freedom in numbers, so I played with great enthusiasm and abandon. If it had been up to me, we'd have had reunions every month.

My favorite game at these gatherings was Cowboys and Indians and Soldiers. We played in the grove of longleaf pines near the house. Using the super-abundant pinecones as ammo, we would divide ourselves into warring camps, build forts, and make endless playful war. I never wanted those days to end.

During a Christmas reunion in 1941, after the big afternoon feast, I was so engrossed in playing war that I didn't go for a spin with a gang of older cousins and my six-year-old sister, Leah, in cousin Suzannah's new Buick convertible. Cousin Sam drove. On the rutted, sandy road, he took a curve too fast and lost control of the car, which flipped over. Suzannah broke her back, Leah's arm was broken above the elbow, Cousin Lois broke a leg, and Sam broke his collarbone. Miraculously, Suzannah recovered completely within a year. I credit my passionate love of those pinecone wars with keeping me safely at home.

I don't know that I had a favorite cousin, but Johnny was certainly one of the most important to me. He was a year or two older than I; in my longing for siblings I sometimes pretended he was my older brother. We were both quite different from our peers: we were non-athletes engaged in activities most other boys would have considered extraordinary; Johnny a zealous scientist, I a performer. We were thrown together most often during that perplexing time when boys turn into men, and it was good to have someone to talk to about the changes overtaking us.

We visited back and forth every summer, a week at his place and a week at mine. Johnny's father, Daddy's brother, Chester, was a plantation manager down at Lake Jackson near Tallahassee. Lake Jackson and the surrounding woods teemed with wildlife and insects. Johnny, fascinated with animals and bugs, would eventually become a renowned entomologist, having always known what he wanted to be when he grew up. I, on the other hand, had always known what I was *supposed* to be when I grew up, and I envied Johnny's passion for something wholly other than the work of his father.

During one visit to Lake Jackson, Johnny and I were settling down to sleep when I heard something scraping and splashing under my bed. I sat up and said, "Johnny, what's that noise?"

"Oh, that's just my pet alligator," he said, yawning. "I keep him in a tub under there. If it bothers you, I'll move him under my bed."

I encouraged him to do so.

When I was twelve and it was determined that I was old

enough to travel by myself, I made the trip to Johnny's home on the coal-powered train that ran through Cottonwood and down to Tallahassee. Just behind the engine was the only car for passengers, and the front half of it was a baggage compartment. I boarded the train wearing an elegant white suit and matching white shoes. In that era prior to the advent of air conditioning, the only way to get fresh air in those cars was to open the windows. Being a warm summer day, many of the windows were open. When I detrained at the country crossroads where Johnny and his mother awaited me, my suit and shoes were black with soot.

When Johnny came to stay with me, our favorite place to hang out was up on the platform around the 5000-gallon water tank that supplied the house, store, and barns with all their water. The installation of that big tank is one of my earliest memories. Daddy fabricated the tank himself, bending and welding together several large sheets of galvanized steel and then placing his creation atop a twenty-foot-high wooden platform. I was four years old when he used several mules and a web of big chains to hoist the tank into place, a dramatic event requiring both engineering know-how and careful handling of the mules.

The tank was filled with water pumped up from the well, and then gravity did the rest—a vast improvement over the earlier, manual means of getting and distributing water. There was a shower beneath the platform, and on hot, humid days we would stand under the falling water, often fully clothed, to gain relief from the oppressive heat.

Johnny and I would climb the ladder to the platform surrounding the tank and sit and talk for hours on end. I don't believe anyone realized how intimate we were, and how we used those private hours to share feelings and concerns and ideas that I certainly didn't share with most other people. Johnny is dead now, murdered for his passport while on an expedition in Mexico.

Our times together on that platform during those long, sultry summer days remain vivid memories.

When Johnny and I talked about our distant futures, imagining ourselves married with children, he a college professor, I a farmer, I was already adamant that I would have several children close together in age, so none of them would feel as lonely as I felt as a child. I remember him nodding thoughtfully to acknowledge the wisdom of my plan.

10
Matriarchs of the Farm

Born white in a deeply segregated society, I was never *told* by my parents that I was superior to black people, nor did I feel so. But the unspoken laws of the racial divide—both literal and psychic—were so fundamental to our daily reality that I knew from a very early age that those of us with pale skin were higher on the pyramid of power than those whose skin was dark. I am sure that on an unconscious level this inequality troubled and saddened me.

We did not refer to African Americans as black, but as *colored*. And though the term is considered politically incorrect today, colored is far more inclusively accurate. For even among black people in the South of that time, the term *black* referred to a person whose skin was literally black, not brown or cream or yellow or honey, to name only a few of the colors used to describe the color of a person's skin.

Babies could care less about the color of the person caring for them; little children must be taught by word and action to fear and mistrust a person because of his or her color. Many of my schoolmates grew up with little or no friendly contact with people of African ancestry, so they feared them, and this fear manifested as disdain and, in some cases, hatred.

I spent my early childhood in a relatively isolated community populated largely by black people. I did not have a black nanny as some Southern gentry did, but I was fed and treated lovingly by Pearl; my de facto nursery was our store, open to people of every shade, and the playmates of my infancy were the children of the quarter.

My father was far more concerned about character than color. His reputation among local whites was that he was too good to the colored people who worked and lived on his land, and that he paid them too well and did too much for them. My mother, for her part, was fascinated with the ongoing dramas of the people of the quarter and our sharecroppers, and she infected me with that same fascination. The upshot of all this was that I liked people—black or white—for who they were. Among my favorite adults from my childhood were the women I will now describe.

I have already spoken of Pearl, our diminutive barefoot cook with whom I shared many a happy moment in the kitchen. She was there bright and early every morning, and went home to her little house in the quarter every day at three. Whenever I think of good country cooking—fatback sizzling in a frying pan—I think of Pearl with her tightly woven braids, her smiling eyes, her open mouth as she laughed, revealing her one gold tooth.

The only other colored woman who came to the house, though she rarely came inside, was Prince Ella, a big, strong woman who did all our laundry, which in the days before washers and dryers was an enormous task. She too lived in the quarter, had no children, and was married to Toot Bradley. Having suffered a serious injury as a young man, Toot dragged one leg as he walked. This meant he had a very limited capacity for work, which put the burden of their bread winning squarely on Prince Ella's formidable shoulders. Perhaps I struck her as pampered compared to the boys of the quarter, or maybe she simply didn't care for children; whatever the cause, Prince Ella did not like me, and it seemed to annoy her greatly that Pearl was fond of me. I, however, liked to hang around and watch her do the laundry, a process I found far more interesting than playing by myself.

Every Monday, Prince Ella would carry all our dirty sheets and soiled clothing out to the wash house where she would boil our laundry in two big cast-iron pots suspended over a wood fire. Then she would rinse the laundry in two twenty-five-gallon galvanized metal washtubs. Washing and rinsing and hanging out the clothes to dry took her all day. On Tuesday, she ironed everything, which again took all day. When she wasn't doing our laundry, she did light fieldwork.

One laundry day when I was five I was left in Prince Ella's care for a few hours. When she took a break to go to her house in the quarter, I followed her. My tagging along infuriated her and she grabbed a switch—a thin stick—and whipped my legs a few times. Naturally, I tattled on her to Mother, who then chastised Prince Ella for having the audacity to strike me.

Prince Ella's reaction to Mother's reprimand was to threaten to quit. When word of her mutiny reached Daddy, he immediately went to make peace with Prince Ella. Knowing what a superlative laundress she was and how difficult it would be to replace her, Daddy appeased her with a slight increase in wages and the promise that she would never have to baby-sit me again. From then on I was afraid of Prince Ella and dreaded her looming presence on Mondays and Tuesdays. Mother continued to complain about Prince Ella's surly attitude, but Daddy would not be moved to dismiss her.

Mary Frances was everything Prince Ella was not. A big-boned, gregarious woman, Mary Frances had twenty-two children with her husband Sebe. Their house was about a mile from ours. To accommodate all those children, Daddy built them a second house next to the first. They were sharecroppers; along with corn and cotton, they raised goats for milk, cheese, and meat. The air surrounding their house was permeated with an overwhelming odor of goat manure mixed with goat urine. I can't stand the smell of goat cheese because it brings back the stench of that place. Nonetheless, Mary Frances's children grew up strong and healthy eating all that goat protein, and with every boy who got old enough to work the land, Sebe was able to plant more cotton. Eventually he had over a hundred acres in cultivation, which meant he was doing well.

Mary Frances loved satin. She had my mother make her several bright satin dresses in red, green, blue, and yellow, and she would wear one of them every Saturday. We would see her coming about one in the afternoon, a brilliant splash of color in the distance, moving barefoot along the dirt track from her place to the store. She would arrive drenched with sweat and take her place on the edge of the porch, legs dangling as she fanned herself with a cardboard fan to keep the flies and gnats off.

Most of the fans that colored folks used came from funeral homes or churches. These fans usually had a colorful scene on one side, and the name of the funeral home or church on the other. Mary Frances would stay there on the porch for hours, visiting and gossiping and laughing. This was her big social event of the week, and she made the most of it, nursing a Royal Crown Orange Crush and sweating profusely in her satin gown, which was really a glorified sack dress.

I felt at ease talking to Mary Francis; indeed, my interactions with the women who came to the store were my first and best lessons in sociability. As I grew more and more comfortable talking to Mary Frances and the other farm matriarchs, I became more self-confident in the world at large. I did not, however, feel such comfort in my conversations with the men of the farm. For the most part they treated me as an extension of Daddy, their boss. Thus a respectful restraint characterized most of my interactions with the males of our community.

Another black woman I enjoyed was Ezzie Lee. She lived in the quarter with her husband, Sunny Hall (not to be confused with the Sonny who shot his wife Ella Mae). Ezzie Lee was very heavy, had an enormous bosom, and wore her short hair braided. She was very friendly to me, and always quick to laugh; and I loved to *make* her laugh. There was, I think, a special joy in our laughing together, an unspoken celebration of our transcending the absurd separatism of our culture.

My most vivid memory of Ezzie Lee was the day I happened to be walking by their house on a Saturday afternoon when Sunny Hall was out chopping wood. Suddenly, Ezzie Lee burst out of the house cursing and screaming at Sunny, grabbed an ax, and lifted it over her head to strike him. I yelled, "No, Ezzie Lee! Don't do that!" When she turned to look in my direction, Sunny took the opportunity to hightail it out of there. I think they'd both been drinking, but in any case I believe I saved Sunny's life or at least spared him a trip to the hospital.

My favorite women of the farm were the sisters Mary Jane and Hazel. To look at them one would never guess they were sisters. Mary Jane was a big woman with enormous feet, dark-skinned, and not particularly pretty. Hazel was tall and slender, her skin honey brown. She was, by any standards, remarkably beautiful.

Mary Jane was childless—she and Prince Ella rarities in that regard—and she lived a fairly stay-at-home life with her husband, Frank, who was a carpenter of sorts and worked for Daddy for day wages. Mary Jane's house was about a mile and a half from the home place and a half mile from Hazel's house.

Hazel lived alone, her husband having died long before I was born. She had one son, Tom, who lived half a mile away from her in the interior of our farm with his wife, Jane, and their four daughters. Those girls had the whitest teeth I have ever seen; I later discovered that the whiteness came from their brushing their teeth with baking soda.

Hazel was, in a word, refined. Her house, her yard, and her regal bearing reflected this. Daddy often stopped at Hazel's for lunch. He told me many times that not only was she a marvelous cook, but also kept her house so clean, scrubbed with potash, that you could eat off the floor. This was easy to believe because Hazel *swept* the yard around her house nearly every day, and did so with such care and intention that the ground resembled a Japanese rock garden, the strokes of her dog-fennel broom leaving artistic swirls and patterns in the soil.

Throughout my childhood and young adulthood, whenever I happened to walk or ride or drive by Hazel's house, I would stop in to speak to her. There was something so genuine and honest and refreshing about her, and she seemed so at peace with herself and her life, that a few minutes in Hazel's presence was an emotional restorative.

Every Monday, Hazel would gather her wash into a big bundle and walk to Mary Jane's with that bundle balanced on her head. She did not steady the load with her hand, but walked straight-backed and graceful, arms swinging in time with her stride. I would later see documentaries of women in Africa carrying loads on their heads in that fashion, with similar grace and ease.

When Hazel got to Mary Jane's, the sisters would spend the day in front of the house in the shade of a huge live oak, doing their wash in a big iron wash pot, boiling their clothes the same way Prince Ella boiled ours. I will carry with me always the picture of those sweet sisters sitting under the generous arms of that great tree, smoking their corncob pipes, talking and laughing, and living peacefully on the Dixon family farm.

    I can feel to the depths of my heart how nurturing and supportive of me these women of color were. Their gestures, their smiles, their interest in me, their praise, their laughter, and their total lack of pretense filled me with love and admiration for them. I have no doubt that my lifelong affinity for older women had its beginnings in my interactions with those women who figured so largely in my childhood.

11
Childhood's Fall

When I was ten, in those last carefree months before the onset of puberty, I found much to enjoy in life. No longer constrained by piano lessons, and having adjusted to wearing glasses, I enjoyed school, had lots of friends and cousins to play with, and had a wonderful connection with my sister Leah. She looked up to me and loved me in a pure and innocent way that was a boon to my ego. But all sweet times come to a close, and in that tenth summer of my childhood, I had an accident that now seems a harbinger of the sexual confusion that would soon befall me.

Our front yard was a perfectly manicured lawn bisected by a cement walkway leading to the front steps. To keep stray livestock from trampling the lawn, Daddy enclosed the yard with a decorative wire fence about three feet high. He built the frame by placing a four-by-four posts about every six feet, with two-by-fours running parallel to the ground as top cap and bottom rung to which the decorative wire was affixed. A wire gate opened onto the cement path, and this gate was held closed by a simple metal latch.

On a warm Sunday afternoon, wanting to show off for Leah, I climbed up on that fence barefoot and walked along the top like a tightrope walker. Leah wanted to try, too, but I said, "No, you're too young yet. When you're older you can."

Then I came to the gate, where Daddy had cut the tops of the posts into steep-sided pyramids to give the entrance a more elegant appearance. To continue my balancing act, I had to step over one of these spearheads and onto the two-by-four that formed the top of the gate frame. Well, the little latch wasn't made to withstand the weight of a ten-year-old boy. When I stepped onto the gate, the latch sprang free, the gate flew open, and I dropped straight down onto that wooden point, which sank deep into my inner thigh an inch from my groin.

I was literally impaled on the fence. I screamed bloody murder and Leah started shrieking. Fortunately, my parents were only a hundred yards from the house. Daddy came running, lifted me off that spike, and carried me up into the house where he laid me on my back on the kitchen table and poured rubbing alcohol into the gaping hole to disinfect the wound.

The puncture was two inches deep, the flesh gouged out, and I was in agony. My parents were always outwardly calm in crisis—Leah was in hysterics—and they bundled me up and drove me to the doctor in Cottonwood for stitches.

When the doctor saw the wound, he said, "No, I'm not going to take any stitches. The hole is too big and deep and the point twisted down in there and lacerated everything. It needs to drain and be totally disinfected." So he gave Mother a big bottle of disinfectant—liquid fire—and she washed out my wound three or four times a day for several days until it began to heal and I could walk again. Every time she poured that stuff in there it burned like hell.

Daddy sawed off the points on the gateposts, blaming himself for my injury, and replaced the wire fence with a board fence. I was happy to see that wire fence go because I felt a twinge every time I looked at it.

Leah, bless her heart, was a little Florence Nightingale while I was laid up. She would stand by the bed, kissing my cheek and holding my hand, saying, "You'll be better soon, Jody."

I suffered no permanent damage from the fall, but as my physical injury receded into the past, a more profound physical challenge unfolded for me: the question of my sexual nature.

One night, when I was eleven, our house was full of visitors and my bedroom was given to a guest. My parents had separate bedrooms, and it was decided that I would spend the night with Daddy in his bed. When I was told I would be sleeping with my father, I became inwardly agitated and excited. I remember getting into bed before him and feeling both fear and elation as I awaited him. This unexpected chance to be so physically close to him unleashed a torrent of feelings in me, and I shivered in anticipation of his lying down beside me.

A modest man, Daddy changed into his pajamas in the bathroom before coming to bed. He climbed in beside me, said goodnight, and was soon asleep. I, however, couldn't sleep. As I lay there in the dark, enveloped in his scent and listening to his somnolent breathing, I became obsessed with the idea of touching his genitals. I lay there in a sweat, yearning to touch him yet fearing to wake him. But when he rolled onto his side so he was facing me and my hand was mere inches from him, I could resist no longer and gently touched him.

In retrospect, after being convinced for most of my life that there was something inherently and terribly wrong with me, I now see little Jody furtively touching that man, his father, as a secret expression of love, nothing more. My father was forbidden to me emotionally and physically, and I longed for him. There is a beautiful emotional logic about my touching my father's genitals.

I did not, in those moments of stolen intimacy, think I was a homosexual. I did not know what that meant in any real sense. I did, however, know that a passion, a fascination, an obsession had been born in me, and I knew that it must be kept secret—a secret that would become a central focus of my consciousness.

I was eleven years old in 1941, in a part of America where homosexuality was a crime, a felony punishable with prison time if you survived the wrath of your neighbors. To Christians—Methodists and Baptists alike—homosexuality was considered an abomination, an unforgivable sin, and an unacceptable affront to God. And though none of this had been explicitly taught to me, the sexual mores of that close-knit, unenlightened society had been psychically transmitted into me every day of my life. Homophobia was not as obvious a phenomenon as racism in the Georgia of my youth, but it was always there; hence my anxiety about feeling effeminate, and the accompanying fear that others might find me so.

After that night with my father—though my inner voice had already begun its persistent chant of "What's wrong with me?"—I became much more ambitious about finding or creating situations in which I could at least catch glimpses of the genitals of boys and men. My outer life may have been all about school and work and growing into a successful, heterosexual manhood, the fulfillment of my parents' expectations, but my inner life was totally dominated by a desire for physical intimacy with other men.

I must add here that I never spoke to anyone about the night I touched my father until I was seventy years old and immersed in therapy. I was lying on my back, sobbing as I revealed this long-hidden truth, reaching out with my hand, desperate for contact.

My therapist asked me, "Are you aware of what you're doing, that you're reaching out to him?"

I sat up and said with great lucidity, "That was about my needing his love, not about sex."

"That's right," said my therapist. "It was not about sex."

12
The Secret Birth

My sister, Dana, was born when I was thirteen. When I tell people that her birth was a complete surprise to me, they assume I mean that my mother's pregnancy was unanticipated. But I am referring to the actual birth, since I never suspected that Mother *was* pregnant. She masked her condition so well that no one but my father knew she was pregnant until two weeks before Dana was born.

Daddy picked Leah and me up after school—a rare event—and on the ride home told us that mother had gone to stay with Granddaddy and Grandmother in Greenville for two weeks. Then he took a long, suspenseful drag on his cigarette and said, "She's going to have a baby, but we don't want you to tell anyone until the baby is born."

My initial reaction was delight. I liked the idea of having another sibling, and was naïve enough about human sexuality not to question the absence of the usual manifestations of a woman "grown large with child." *How* Mother managed to cover the evidence isn't half as telling as *why*.

My mother was five feet two inches and not naturally inclined to slenderness. Her tendency to roundness in no way lessened her desire to appear trim and stylish at all times. She declared her ideal weight to be 132 pounds, and if ever she tipped the scales at 135, she would loudly and frequently declare a state of emergency until dieting brought her weight down. As far as

I know she never topped 139 in her life except when she was secretly pregnant with Dana.

After my second little sister came home safe and sound from the hospital, Mother proudly reported that she had gained only ten pounds during the pregnancy, that her dresses had increased by only one size, and that she had diligently worn her girdle so no one would suspect her condition. Indeed, when Dana was born, but before Mother brought her home, Daddy gave us permission to share the glad tidings at church, which we did. Yet no one believed us, which was quite embarrassing to me.

But *why* had Mother gone to such lengths to conceal her pregnancy, even from her own children? Because my mother, in truth, did not want to be pregnant again. In those days, women her age, thirty-eight, did not as a general rule get pregnant, except by accident. Anything approaching forty was considered far too old. Mother did not want to appear fat or weak or dependent; she wanted to see herself and be seen by others as a smart, stylish, independent woman. Appearances were of the utmost importance to my mother, often more important than the truth.

After my mother died, I learned that it had been my father's idea for them to have another child. He wanted another son, because it had become obvious to him that I was not shaping up to be his ideal successor. Mother was little interested in his plan, until he enticed her with the promise of a new mink stole. Upon Dana's birth, Daddy delivered the prize to Mother in the hospital.

As if that scenario weren't sad enough, when Mother came home from the hospital she took the stole to the furrier and had it appraised. When she learned it was *real* mink worth over $500—a fortune in 1943—she immediately traded it in for a mink-dyed squirrel stole and cash. In revealing all this to me, Daddy concluded the story of Dana's birth by saying that Mother's cashing in the stole had crushed him.

Despite these painful moments in my parents' continuing rivalry, I was happy to have a new sister. Her presence brightened my life ever after. And Daddy, realizing that it was now a virtual certainty that I was going to be the *only* son he would ever have, decided to make the best of the situation and focus a little more attention on me. Dana's birth coincided with the beginning of my involvement with Future Farmers of America, which gave my father hope that I might yet prove a viable heir.

I didn't feel then and I don't feel now that there was any malice toward me in Daddy's desire to have another son, though I'm sure I subliminally registered this attempt at begetting another son as a rejection of me. Daddy was single-minded, which was a large part of his success. His overriding motivation in all things was to do what he felt would further the fortunes of the farm. Whether another son would have fared differently than I under Mother's care will never be known. My parents may have been more enlightened than most of their peers, but they too were products of their hardscrabble childhoods, and therefore ambitious, in very pragmatic ways, for themselves and their children.

13
Travels with Daddy

As far back as I can remember, I've had an insatiable appetite for new experiences. I learned from my father that travel was the surest way to feed that craving. Daddy and Granddaddy both loved adventure, and I inherited their zeal for going places to see the wonders and curiosities outside our little corner of the world. We traveled extensively throughout my childhood; by the time I graduated from high school I had been to forty-five of the forty-eight states. We went by car, train, and boat, and eventually by airplane. Sometimes the entire family traveled together, sometimes either Mother or Daddy stayed home to watch over the farm while the rest of us took a trip.

My father planned our travels in the same intense and meticulous way he managed the farm. Spontaneity and improvisation were rare when Daddy was in charge. Nonetheless, everything along the way was thrilling to me.

Mother was much more spontaneous and relaxed when we were on the road. Despite my parents' reticence with each other, I loved it when we all traveled together and were held closer than ever in the embrace of our car. I think it fair to say that Daddy and Mother enjoyed each other more while traveling. They certainly spoke more freely to each other and used me less often as their go-between.

My father smoked as he drove. Sitting in the back seat, it became my habit to open my window a little to give myself some relief from the incredibly stuffy atmosphere. When I continued to crack the window after the advent of air conditioning, my father would quip in his caustic way, "You trying to cool the outdoors, too?" Rather than reveal my aversion to his smoke, a revelation I felt would have been disrespectful, I would roll up my window, wait a few minutes, and then ever so subtly roll it down again.

On one of our many trips through the mountains of north Georgia, we were driving up Bald Mountain, the highest peak in the state, the narrow road paralleling a sparkling stream. It was a gorgeous day, sunlight glinting off the water, and Mother said, "Oh Harvey, stop. I want to get my feet in that water." Daddy resisted for a moment, having not planned for such frivolity, but Mother persisted and he pulled over to the side of the road. We all took off our shoes and dangled our feet in the rushing stream. Daddy took a picture of Mother and Leah and me, all of us smiling blissfully. I think I was eleven, Leah six.

Not that Daddy couldn't occasionally be spontaneous: I remember a Saturday at noon on a blazing-hot summer day, when Daddy came riding up on his horse and said, "Let's go down to Panama City." An hour later we were ready to go, the car gassed up, the windshield sparkling clean. Daddy *never* left home with a dirty windshield, and neither do I. The drive to Panama City, our favorite coastal destination, took three hours.

We got a room with two double beds in Panama City's finest downtown hotel. When we rose the next day, Daddy thrilled us all by calling room service and ordering breakfast. This was an unprecedented event. I have rarely felt so special and pampered as I felt that morning as we dined in our pajamas.

Daddy's love affair with the north Georgia mountains began when he was thirteen and spent a year at a Methodist boarding school in the town of Young Harris. For those nine months he lived at Mrs. Thompson's boarding house, a place he described as a veritable Valhalla of good food amidst the sweet splendor of those glorious mountains. When I was ten, we made a pilgrimage to visit Mrs. Thompson, and all of Daddy's recollections proved to be true.

Mrs. Thompson, a short, broad-beamed woman with a smile as big as her dahlias, engulfed Daddy in a loving hug, gave me a hug, too, and then served us fried chicken with all the fixings—a meal to die for!

From a child's perspective, our most exotic abode in those mountains was the house we rented in Mountain City. The little bungalow was built *over* a stream. That was the first time I ever encountered a lazy Susan—on the dining table in the kitchen—and the only time I've ever seen a refrigerator of the sort we had there. Imagine a trapdoor in the kitchen floor through which the cooling box could be hoisted up from its resting place in the waters below. Unfortunately, that was also the vacation during which I contracted malaria and spent most of my days in bed sipping quinine.

A favorite family pastime in Panama City was deep-sea fishing. Mother loved to fish. Daddy preferred hunting, but he fished, too, along with Granddaddy and any of the cousins who wanted to go along. There was no fancy sonar on board for locating fish, only the skipper's wiles to guide us. We caught grouper and snapper, along with the occasional shark.

I will never forget the day we were out fishing, the boat rising and falling on an unusually large swell, when all of a sudden Granddaddy vomited and his false teeth came flying out of his mouth. With amazing dexterity, he caught his teeth in midair before they could hit the water. He was deeply embarrassed and went below to clean up.

Granddaddy's return to the deck after the humiliation of throwing up in front of us is one of my most sharply etched memories of him. He was an intensely proud man, stern and tough. Though he was still terribly seasick, he stood on deck, no longer fishing, determined that we see him as unbowed and undefeated.

To celebrate his eightieth birthday, Granddaddy prompted an expedition to San Francisco to see the World's Fair. He wanted to visit the city Daddy loved more than any other, so he and Grandmother, Daddy, Cousin Mary Lucille, and I took the train cross-country. The roundtrip lasted seventeen days, fourteen of which we spent on the train. We stayed two nights in a hotel in San Francisco and had a whirlwind day at the World's Fair. Our only other night off the train was in the grand lodge at Yellowstone Park. We caught a glimpse of Old Faithful and once again boarded the train.

Grandmother was always so quiet, I never knew if she was enjoying herself, but I recall Granddaddy laughing more than usual on that trip, so I think he must have been having a good time. Dorothy Jane and I amused ourselves by roaming up and down the train, playing cards, and watching Granddaddy sleep. He would put his head back, mouth agape, and snore. The flies would buzz around, coming closer and closer to his open mouth until a big exhalation would blow them all away. Dorothy Jane and I would laugh in delight at this performance.

In 1939, Daddy and Granddaddy made what in those days was considered an epic journey to New York City. They traveled to the Big Apple by boat from Savannah and returned by airplane to Atlanta. Daddy liked to tell about their arrival in Times Square, and how Granddaddy tilted his head back and turned slowly in a circle, mouth agape in amazement at the sight of all the skyscrapers.

On their last night in Manhattan, Daddy woke in the middle of the night and found Granddaddy's bed empty. Fearing the worst, Daddy dressed quickly and hurried out to look for his father. He found him standing on a nearby street corner, eating an ice-cream cone and gazing at the sparkling lights of the city.

"What are you doing out here?" asked Daddy.

"I just wanted to see what the city looked like at midnight," said Granddaddy, licking his cone. Then he sighed and said, "Last night here, don't want to miss anything."

Then they laughed, and they would laugh again whenever my father told that story. Their laughing together made a big impression on me. I interpreted it to mean that travel was emotional elixir and could make hard men softer; the antithesis of routine and the antidote to sorrow, travel was more than escape, but a marvelously unpredictable form of magic.

Daddy adopted Granddaddy's ritual of buying an ice-cream cone wherever he traveled. When he was in his late eighties, Daddy and I took a trip to California. In Santa Cruz we stopped at an ice-cream parlor with a Help Wanted sign in the window. Daddy, an inveterate flirt, entered, approached the middle-aged woman behind the counter, bowed gallantly, and said with his gentlemanly Georgia drawl, "Ah would very much like to help you in any capacity you desire." The woman was happy to flirt with him, sensing no threat from the old man having fun at the end of his life.

14
Rites of Passage

Both my parents were excellent marksmen, and gave me my first BB gun when I was ten. Shooting became a frequent afternoon pastime for me, mostly in the pecan orchard, my prey being birds and squirrels, though one time I went after bigger game, and thereby hangs the following tale.

We had a two-acre pond where I sometimes went to shoot. One afternoon when I was eleven, I wandered down to the pond and came upon a huge gray migrating goose. I shot at him from a distance and could see from his reaction that I'd hit him in the head with my little BB. I expected him to fly away, but he stayed where he was. As I approached him, I continued to shoot, hitting him several more times; but for some reason he held his ground. When I got to within ten feet of him, he shook his bloody head, let out a wild honking scream, and charged me. Terrified, I grabbed the barrel of my gun and swung the butt at him, striking him again and again until he dropped dead.

When I caught my breath and my heart stopped pounding, I experienced a wave of sadness that quickly gave way to Dixon pragmatism. I surmised that I couldn't bring the bloody bird home—too messy—but I *was* curious to see how he tasted, so I carried him to Pearl's house in the quarter and asked if she would cook him for me. When I told her she could have him, that I just wanted a taste, she was delighted. I watched her pluck, skin, and gut the big bird, and then she fried a chunk of the flesh in pork fat. I found it tough, gamy, and greasy. Pearl pronounced it delicious and thanked me for bringing such a boon to her larder.

On my twelfth birthday, Daddy gave me a twenty-gauge automatic shotgun and I became a much deadlier shot than ever before. I kept my guns in the custom-made gun cabinet that Daddy built into the wall of my new bedroom. He loved to hunt and he very much wanted me to love it, too. Later in life, I realized that I didn't actually like killing things, but because I was expected to, and it was proof of masculinity, I did my share of killing.

Shortly thereafter, my mother decided I should become a Boy Scout. There was no troop in Cottonwood, which meant I would have to travel to Greenville for meetings and field trips. Mother's decision that I become a scout was no doubt influenced by my father's desire to send me away to a military academy for high school, an idea Mother vehemently opposed.

I didn't learn of my father's wish to militarize my education until I was fifty. My father, then seventy-five years old, was in one of his confessional phases when he told me that he felt guilty about not being more available to me when I was a child. He explained that he'd always been uncomfortable with babies and little children and had made the following agreement with Mother: "You raise the kids, I'll run the farm." He went on to say that his wish to send me to a military academy sprang from his desire to "make a man of me." Having bequeathed control of me to Mother for the duration of my childhood, he reasoned that by sending me away to a military academy I would no longer be under Mother's direct control, and my more manly attributes would then be able to assert themselves.

I remember trying to absolve him of any blame by saying, "You did the best you knew how, Daddy," but I deeply resented his continuous abandonment of me throughout my childhood and adolescence.

Regardless of why I became a scout—the lone scout of Mitchell County—those two years of scouting were great. I attended a summer camp where I learned to swim, and one of my more heroic deeds took place while I was earning a merit badge for outdoor cooking.

A friend and I were camping beside the local swimming hole on little Cypress Creek, not far from the home place. We were cooking our meal on an open fire, a requirement for earning that merit badge. We cooked eggs and sausage on a cast-iron griddle, served up our meals into our Boy Scout mess kits, and then took my scout hatchet and went to gather more firewood. Upon returning to our camp, I found a large king snake slithering away, a sausage in his mouth.

Without hesitating, I took aim and threw my hatchet at him. To my astonishment and delight, I not only hit him, but the hatchet blade split the snake's head in two and pinned the carcass to the ground! I never tired of recounting my Daniel Boone-like exploit, though few people ever believed me.

In the world I grew up in, heroics were accomplished on the

playing field or through daredevil antics, fist fighting, or hunting. Academic achievement and success in business would count for much more later in life, but as a boy becoming a man in southern Georgia in the 1940s, visceral deeds mattered most. Since I was not an athlete, a daredevil, or a fighter, my skill with a rifle was my most overtly masculine talent.

When I was fourteen and daily oppressed by the feeling that I was a big disappointment to my father, I was thrilled when he asked me to undertake the shooting of seventy-five grade-one hogs for the winter slaughter. I remember him saying to me at supper the night before, "Well, the weather has turned cold enough now, so you can stay home from school tomorrow and you can take the rifle. You're a good enough shot now, so I'll trust you to lay the hogs down."

This slaughter was a rite of passage—my official entry into manhood—and was a much more difficult undertaking than you might imagine. I had won a 4-H Club turkey shoot when I was twelve, shooting at a stationary target 200 feet away, and had shot squirrels, a raccoon, an opossum, and even a few speedy rabbits. But shooting seventy-five big hogs, each animal weighing 200 pounds, was a task requiring the steadiest of hands and a cool head.

The slaughter and butchering of the hogs was an all-day operation involving at least two dozen people working a complicated assembly line of tables and tubs. The process began with killing the hog and then scalding the carcass in a huge cast-iron tub, scraping the hair off the skin, hanging the hog upside-down, gutting it, catching the innards in a big galvanized tub, cutting off the head to be ground up for headcheese, cutting up the carcass and removing the prime cuts to the smokehouse or the icehouse, cleaning the intestines to make casings for sausages, grinding up meat from the lesser cuts to make the sausages, gathering the fatback for cooking, pickling the feet and the ears, and preparing the chitterlings for sale. And those are only the *main* parts of the process.

Mother oversaw the making of sausages, seasoning the meat—ground in a hand-cranked grinder—with black pepper, salt, and sage, and then frying test patties right on the spot to make sure she had the flavoring right. When she was satisfied with the combination of spices, the manufacture of sausage continued—a process involving another hand-cranked contraption that filled the cleaned intestines with the ground meat. The work of harvesting the hogs often lasted into the night, and Daddy would bring up trucks to illuminate the site with headlights. Each of the families who helped in the process got to carry away a big load of meat and fat and sausages.

It was my job on that momentous day to "lay the hogs down" with a single shot from a .22 that would enter the hog's brain an inch above the center point between the eyes. A perfectly accurate shot would drop the hog immediately. If the bullet missed the mark by as little as a quarter inch, the hog would go crazy, charging and thrashing around the pen, often requiring several more shots to effect a kill.

Imagine a pen containing twenty hogs. The shooter enters the pen and moves around until he is facing a hog at a distance of about fifteen feet—any closer and the hog will run away. The shooter raises the rifle, takes aim, holds his breath, and fires. Assuming the shot is accurate, the hog keels over and ceases to move. Now the shooter confronts the next hog, fires again, and continues until all the hogs have been dispatched. When the bodies have been removed from the pen, twenty more hogs are brought in. It's not easy, even for a seasoned expert.

I barely slept the night before, anxiously visualizing myself in the role of the shooter. The scene was familiar, so it was a matter of imagining myself calm and steady as I worked. All the people involved in the hog harvest—especially Daddy—would be watching or listening as I shot the hogs, and a bad shot would cause a hog to squeal so loud it might as well have been a siren sounding.

As it happened, I had a steady hand all morning. I dropped seventy-three out of seventy-five with the first shot. The other two hogs required only one more shot to finish them. Few men had ever been so successful, and Daddy was pleased with me. His approval was of immeasurable importance—an acknowledgment that I was now worthy of his trust.

I'm sure Mother was pleased, too. This particular slaughter would have taken place when Daddy was still pushing to send me to a military academy; my accomplishment would have aided my mother's argument that I was progressing well enough at home.

Daddy had given Mother oversight of the harvesting of our sixty-acre pecan orchard. As the profits from the sale of the pecans were hers to do with as she pleased, protecting the pecan crop from marauding crows and squirrels was one of Mother's regular pursuits.

I remember once going to investigate the plaintive squawking of a crow out in the orchard. I found Mother, perfectly groomed and in a stylish dress as always, standing with her foot on the wounded bird, prodding it to make sounds of distress to attract other crows for her to shoot with her twenty-gauge shotgun. I was shocked by her casual brutality, but I understood her motives. Mother was determined to be optimally successful, and every pecan eaten by a crow diminished her profits.

One of the most memorable expenditures of Mother's pecan money was the year she bought Leah a splendid Hammond organ, for which Daddy built a music alcove adjoining the living room. The alcove housed the organ and a spinet piano, and though by high school I'd forgotten most of what I learned during my year of piano lessons, I could pick out single notes on the organ while my much more skillful sister accompanied me on the piano.

One of the culinary high points of my life took place whenever the hog slaughter happened to coincide with the grinding of the sugarcane in the late fall. Coming home from school to the intoxicating smell of frying sausage, I would drop my books, get a plate of cold biscuits from Pearl, and go out to the assembly line where Mother was testing her sausage patties. I would put a few sizzling patties on top of the biscuits and then run down to the sugarcane mill where they were filling one-gallon tin cans with warm cane syrup. I would take one of the big tin lids, catch a good pool of syrup on it, and then sit in a corner, sopping my biscuits and sausage in the thick, sweet syrup. If that description doesn't make your mouth water, you're not from the South.

I must admit that I never once tasted the headcheese we had for sale in the store, though I sold thousands of slices—two for a nickel—to colored people who considered it a delicacy superior even to pickled pigs feet, pickled pigs ears, and chitterlings. Virtually no part of the hog was wasted. According to the unwritten Dixon creed, wasting anything was a sin, and everything my impressively competent parents did reinforced that imperative in me.

15
Acting Out

Mitchell County High was just across the street from Cottonwood Elementary. This meant that the routine of coming and going to school barely changed when I started high school, though everything else was radically different. For one thing, our high school was consolidated, which meant that it was attended by the Cottonwood town kids and by all the farm kids in the county. The social order of the school, with few exceptions, divided along that line of town and country. In keeping with the laws of that time and place, there were no people of color at our school.

I belonged to a group of kids that had coalesced in elementary school: eight girls and three boys, exclusively town kids save for me. All of the girls I dated in high school came from this group. I remain friends with each of them — those among the living — to this day. In my heart of hearts I considered myself one of the farm kids, though most of my friends were from town.

Every Friday night we had a dance in town, and I rarely missed a chance to dance. We convened at The Clubhouse — a little old veteran's building — with a phonograph and a stack of 78s. To make choosing a partner carefree and equitable, we would form a circle, boy-girl-boy-girl; someone would call out, "Two to your right," or "Four to your left," and the boys would move to the girl at that position. In this way, even the geeks and the wallflowers got a chance to dance.

I was gifted with a great sense of rhythm, and dancing was my bliss, so those Friday nights were heaven. We did the two-step with every variation imaginable, the jitterbug, and the shag. Anybody who learned a new step would teach it to the rest of us. Dancing was my sport, though I wouldn't have known to call it that at the time, and I reveled in my prowess on the floor. When I danced, I felt strong, purposeful, and masculine, for there was nothing at all weak or tentative or girlish in the way I handled my partners.

Though I liked girls and assumed I would eventually bed and wed one of them, my fascination with the sexual equipment of males continued to obsess me. It became my constant habit to furtively check out the below-the-waist contours of every male I encountered, hoping to glimpse a promising bulge. In church I would be assailed by guilt about my sinfulness, and prayed fervently to be freed from my obsession, for I felt utterly helpless to overcome it by myself. I had not yet acted out my fantasies in any way since the night I touched my father, but I thought of little else.

Then one day after school, I went with two other boys to a fourth boy's apartment in Cottonwood. We ended up in his bedroom, sitting on the bed, talking about the girls we liked — who was the cutest, who was the sexiest — and one of the guys started rubbing himself and saying, "Oh that feels good." I could hardly believe my luck.

One by one we unzipped and masturbated en masse. In short order we had our collective orgasm, and thereafter, any time I spent the night with one or more of these particular boys, we masturbated together, usually at my instigation. But we never touched each other. That was forbidden.

I soon came to realize that most boys my age were exploring the ejaculatory aspects of sex with their male friends, with nary a whiff of homosexuality connected to these investigations. Nearly all the initiating talk was of girls and wanting to have sex with them. But for me, in the privacy of my mind, being with other boys in this way was far more than experimentation; it was fuel for my obsession. I had to constantly reign in my eagerness to initiate these sessions, for fear of being thought of as queer, though I was not fully certain what being queer was.

Meanwhile, I became a cheerleader, something virtually unheard of for a male in those days. Several of the girls in our group were the official cheerleaders of our high school, and since I went to all the basketball games with them it naturally evolved that I would cheer with them. I was such a big ham that any embarrassment I may have felt in this traditionally female role was overwhelmed by my desire to strut my stuff in front of a crowd. Besides, it was a great release for me to yell and shout and jump around in the midst of all that wild pubescent energy in a high school gym.

Along with cheerleading, I had lead roles in all the plays, almost always opposite one or another of my group of girlfriends. We went to district and state competitions, which made for wonderful breaks from the tedium of farm life. In some parts of America, acting in plays may have been considered a sissy thing for boys, but in my day at Mitchell County High, getting up in front of all those people and never forgetting a line was, thank God, considered a brave endeavor.

I'm not sure what Daddy thought of my non-farming activities, but Mother enjoyed my being in the spotlight, so long as my clothes looked good and my hair was just right. I participated in speech competitions sponsored by Future Farmer of America, and Daddy was always supportive of any activity underwritten by that organization. He might have come to see me in plays, but I have no memory of him ever being there.

Known in the larger community as a gifted performer, I was asked by a teacher, Katherine Fairfax, to recite the last lines of the famous poem *Thanatopsis* at her husband's funeral.

I remember those lines to this day, an admonition I heartily agree with.

> *So live, that when thy summons comes to join*
> *The innumerable caravan which moves*
> *To that mysterious realm, where each shall take*
> *His chamber in the silent halls of death,*
> *Thou go not, like the quarry-slave at night,*
> *Scourged to his dungeon, but, sustained and soothed*
> *By an unfaltering trust, approach thy grave*
> *Like one who wraps the drapery of his couch*
> *About him, and lies down to pleasant dreams.*

So I carved for myself a place in the society of my peers that fueled my self-esteem and fulfilled my love of drama and excitement. And there was another great benefit to my numerous extracurricular activities: time away from the farm and the formidable weight of parental expectations.

16
Enemies

I was eleven years old when the United States entered World War II, and nearly sixteen when the war ended. While Europe suffered horrifically during those years, and the war deeply impacted American life, our little corner of the planet actually benefited from the global conflagration. Men who had been out of work during the Depression joined the army or found jobs in the suddenly awakened economy, while Daddy continued to expand Joleda Farm both in acreage and with the introduction of registered Hereford cattle and Tennessee Walkers—a sought-after breed of pleasure horse.

In 1944, in order to build the grand horse barn that would be the center of his new equine operations, Daddy took advantage of a most unusual government resource: German prisoners-of-war. The air force base some twenty miles away at Cambridge had been transformed into a camp for German POWs; these men were for hire at the unbeatable price of a dollar a day. All we had to do was fetch them at seven in the morning and have them back to the camp by five in the evening. The government even provided their lunches and a security guard.

Daddy outfitted a one-and-a-half-ton truck with benches and high sideboards to transport the prisoners. Every day for seven months spanning a spring and a summer, we had twenty or so German men on the farm. They were strong, hardworking, generally good-natured, and glad to be doing something other than waiting out their days in the camp barracks. Our dreaded foes turned out to be friendly, cooperative, homesick, and blameless—victims of the madness of their rulers.

Before he undertook construction of the horse barn, Daddy tested the prisoners with the task of clearing pine forest for cultivation. The trees were felled and hauled to the sawmill, then the stumps, eighteen to thirty inches in diameter, had to be removed. We used a bulldozer to rip out the big stumps and push them into piles for burning. But the POWs were so quick and strong that they didn't wait for the bulldozer to gather the stumps. The moment a stump was loose, two of the Germans would swarm to it and carry it between them to the pile.

Their strength and energy amazed me. Our day workers were every bit as strong as the Germans, but most of them were going to be farm workers for the rest of their lives—in it for the long haul—so they worked at a much slower, steadier pace than these German strangers in a strange land. I came to like the POWs so well that I ceased to think of them as enemies. Indeed, I looked forward to their arrival in the morning and spent many a day in their company, especially once work began on the horse barn.

I learned a tiny bit of German during their time on the farm—*guten morgen, guten tag*—and I learned to swear, too, though they discouraged my use of bad words. There was never any worry that they would escape; there was no place for them to escape *to*. And, as much as any prisoners could, they seemed to enjoy working for Daddy.

The barn they built for us was quite large: a hundred feet long and thirty feet wide. Made of concrete block, the building consisted of a wide center hall off of which were fourteen single stalls built of our homegrown pine. There was a one-story shed, twelve feet wide, that ran the length of the backside of the barn, a tack room, a feed room, a wash rack, and pull-down stairs to get up to the vast hayloft.

When the barn was nearly finished, one of the prisoners informed Daddy that he was a skilled calligrapher and wanted to paint the names of the horses on plaques to go over their respective stalls. Daddy was delighted. Those beautifully rendered names—Judge, Jimmy, Lazy Bones, Nellie, White Child, Ellen, Sylvia, Mac, to name a few—added a further touch of class to his already classy operation.

One of the more bizarre aspects of having German POWs in our midst was their undisguised contempt for the black people on the farm; they absolutely refused to work or interact with them. And we bowed to their wishes in this regard! Even though they were our sworn enemies and prisoners, we acknowledged their social superiority to our own loyal farm hands. The Germans were white—not white trash—strong, attractive, and hardworking. Racism, apparently, was even more deeply ingrained in us than nationalism.

Yes, even in the midst of war, with terrifying dehumanized enemies we called Krauts and Japs, the Deep South remained as primitively racist as ever. The year before we hired the POWs, Miss Mary Johns, an elderly widow who lived in the white community of Johnstown, about three miles from the home place, was found dead in her back yard. Word spread that she had been raped and strangled and that her yard had been dug up. It was said she kept her money in a jar buried in the ground, so it was surmised the killer was looking for her money.

Suspicion fell on the retarded and somewhat disabled black man who ran errands and did yard work for Miss Mary. There was no proof he was involved, but that didn't stop a posse of angry white men from going in search of him. The moment Daddy got news of Mary's death, he hurried down to the quarter and told everyone that Mary Johns had been raped and murdered and that white men were out to avenge her death. He told everyone in the quarter to stay home until he gave the all clear. Then he jumped in his truck and drove to the homes of all the colored families living on or near our land to give them the same warning. The next day, the posse of white men found that poor retarded man, chained him by the ankle to the back of a truck, and dragged him along the road until he was dead and pulverized.

Going to such lengths to protect colored people only added to Daddy's reputation as a "nigger lover," but he never cared what less-enlightened people thought of him. He was being pragmatic, too, not wanting any of his workers injured or killed.

The people who worked for Daddy revered him; this reverence usually, though not always, extended to me. By the time I was fourteen, Daddy had me straw bossing, as we called it, acting as foreman on various jobs around the farm. I hadn't earned my stripes working in the fields, but was given a position of authority by virtue of being my father's son and heir apparent.

Almost every morning, my father would stand on the store porch and give the work orders for the day. One time early in my straw-bossing career, Daddy said to me, "The holding pens over by the dent pond need repair. Get some new boards at the mill." Then he told me which tools I would need and which truck to use. Then he said, "Horace, you and J.C. go with Jody."

Horace and J.C. were bachelors, older farm hands, and shared a little place in the quarter. Horace was six feet tall, muscular, and in his forties; J.C. was shorter and in his fifties. They both wore overalls with no shirt underneath, brogan shoes, and no socks. I drove them to the mill, told them which boards to load, and then we drove to the field near the dent pond, a circular body of water, never dry, about three feet deep and covering some four acres. I told them what we needed to do and they got to work. But after just a few minutes, Horace threw down his hammer and said, "I ain't takin' no orders from you. You ain't a man."

J.C. thought about this for a minute, threw down his hammer, too, and they started walking back to the store. My first thought was, "I've let Daddy down. I failed." My second thought was, "I wonder if he'll be mad at me?"

I loaded the tools and nails into the truck and headed home. "May as well ride back as walk," I said when I caught up to Horace and J.C. They scowled at me for a moment and then climbed into the back of the truck. When we got back to the store, Daddy wasn't around. Not wanting to further damage my reputation as a straw boss, I told them as calmly as I could, "If you're not gonna work, go on home."

Daddy came in a few minutes later and said, "Don't tell me you finished already."

I told him what had happened. He thought for a moment and said, "Well, let 'em miss a day's wages then." He wasn't the least bit critical of me, for which I was grateful.

The next morning, in front of everybody, Daddy spoke firmly to J.C. and Horace, telling them that if they ever defied me again they would no longer work or live on our farm. Then he sent us back to do the job, which we did, though Horace and J.C. were sullen and silent the whole day.

In retrospect, it is easy to understand why seasoned farm

hands, especially men so much older than I, would resent being bossed by a fourteen-year-old kid with little hands-on experience. Yet at the time I found their attitude perplexing and annoying. I remember asking Daddy at the end of that frustrating day, "How do you have the patience to work with them?"

To which he replied in his matter-of-fact way, "Because I make good money from them."

Thereafter, I never straw bossed J.C. or Horace again. There were plenty of younger farm hands who had no problem with me overseeing their work, and Daddy tried to avoid conflict whenever possible.

One afternoon I came home from high school, dropped my books, and went to the kitchen for a snack. Mother came in carrying Dana, my adorable baby sister, and asked me to mind the store while she went to town. I finished my snack and sauntered down to the store, and as I entered I heard something that sounded like a herd of rats charging around in the corn bin.

I tiptoed to the back of the store where we kept our bulk grains in big wooden bins, and there, in one of the bins, was our white bookkeeper having sex with one of the colored women from the quarter—Pearl's daughter. I was shocked to see a white man atop a colored woman, but I was also greatly aroused by the scene. I only watched for a moment, until the woman's eyes met mine, and then I turned away, never telling anyone what I'd witnessed.

A wartime trip to buy bulls looms large in my memory. In 1942, Mother, Daddy, Leah, and I traveled the many hundreds of miles to Oklahoma in our '41 Buick, no small feat given that gas, tires, and sugar were being rationed. To make the trip, Daddy saved up his coupons for gas and retreads, and bought coupons from folks who needed money more than gas. Daddy had to be careful that all such transactions were absolutely legal because he was on the county ration board. Cheating of any kind was severely frowned upon.

This was one trip where Daddy's meticulous planning was absolutely essential to our success because we would be going where service stations were few and far between. The roads in Oklahoma were narrow, and for long stretches they followed the perfectly straight edges of huge land holdings and would come to abrupt right angles as they followed the rectangular forms of the parcels.

One day at dusk near Durant, Oklahoma, on just such a sharp-cornered road, we were pulled over by the local sheriff. He shined his flashlight into the back seat where Leah and I sat huddled together, frowning in fear. It seems that a little girl Leah's age had disappeared, and here we were with Georgia plates in the middle of nowhere, the war on, gas being rationed—suspicious!

After Daddy convinced the sheriff we were not kidnapers, we drove into Durant and found a motor court where we got a little cabin with two double beds. We were nearly out of food, hungry, and we needed a new retread. Daddy left us in the cabin and went out to see what he could find. He returned two hours later having secured the tire and this repast: a gallon of milk, a bunch of bananas, and a box of saltine crackers. Mother, always fearing for our health and doubting the sanitary standards of our hosts, insisted that we wear our socks while walking on the cabin floor, and that we then remove our socks to sit on the bed, where she determined we would have our feast.

Supper over, we lay down to sleep. A few minutes later, I heard someone scratching himself in the other bed. Then the scratching stopped, started again, grew quite furious, then stopped, only to start again. A moment later, Mother jumped up, turned on the light and said, "Harvey, there are bedbugs!"

Daddy was laughing so hard he could barely breathe. There were no bedbugs, but his scratching had convinced Mother there were, and she had begun to feel those imaginary bugs crawling on her skin. We children didn't dare laugh at Mother, though we wanted to, and Daddy laughed at his trick for a long time after.

Thinking back to the war years, I recall how the sexual battle within me continued to rage. Everything that happened to me had its carnal aspect. When the German soldiers would strip off their shirts to labor in the heat, I found myself aroused by their beautiful bodies. When I danced close to my pretty girlfriends in The Clubhouse, I was aroused by their touch and how their bodies moved with mine. Everywhere I looked there were animals mating, lovers kissing, and people looking at me, their eyes seeming to ask the most important questions of all: Who are you, Jody, and what are you going to do about it?

17
Daddy's Bull

At the close of World War II, my father decided to upgrade his herd of Herefords by purchasing a registered bull from a prominent breeding herd to breed with his non-registered cows. Daddy always thought big; his goal was to eventually have only the finest registered Herefords grazing on his land. So he drove to Beeville, Oklahoma, and bought a senior breeding bull named Hazlett from the renowned rancher Curtis Hazlett. Daddy wrote Curtis a check for the agreed-upon sum and then drove home to make arrangements for the arrival of the bull.

He went to his banker in Cottonwood and said, "Martin, I need to borrow ten thousand dollars."

"Certainly, Harvey," said Martin. "No problem. May I ask what you'll be using the money for?"

Daddy's Bull

"I bought a bull," said Daddy.

Martin's eyes bugged out. "For ten thousand dollars? Have you lost your mind?"

Daddy replied, "I hope not. I already wrote the check."

Word spread like wildfire that Harvey Dixon had paid the incredible sum of $10,000 for a bull. Naturally, everyone for miles around wanted a good look at that animal. Ever the entrepreneur, Daddy built a stylish little pavilion where Hazlett, who weighed over a ton, would be enthroned upon arrival. News of the purchase was in all the local and regional papers; people came not only from neighboring counties, but also from neighboring states to view the mythic bull. Once again, Daddy was breaking new ground in the Old South.

At two and a half years old, Hazlett had yet to prove himself a sire worth so colossal an investment. There were many doubters, of course, but once again Daddy's intuition paid off. Hazlett succeeded abundantly. Daddy then bought thirty purebred cows with pedigrees selected to mate well with Hazlett. From the resulting offspring he created a herd of outstanding brood cows. These female offspring became sought after all over the Southeast as "foundation breeding mothers," and Hazlett's sons were popular sires in the Southeast commercial herd market—herds of non-registered crossbreeds.

Several planeloads of Joleda bulls were flown to Costa Rica to improve the quality of beef production there. Then Daddy bought even better bulls to breed with Hazlett's daughters, and thus was born one of the preeminent herds in America. The doubters disappeared, and Daddy became recognized as a front runner in the America Hereford Association. He loved the recognition, and he deserved every bit of it.

Hazlett continued to breed successfully until he was twelve years old. Then, ironically, while attempting to do what he had done so well for so long, he aimed high, thrust forward, and literally broke his baby maker on the unyielding pelvic bone of the cow. Bellowing in agony, he fell to the ground and lay unmoving for a month; when he was finally recovered enough to rise, he never bred again. We hated to give up on him, because he was such a regal beast and had meant so much to the farm, but there was little point in prolonging his suffering.

Around the time we got Hazlett, I had one of my closer calls with death. I was walking home from visiting Aunt Sally, when one of the farm hands came along driving a tractor towing a rotary mower. I jumped onto the back of the tractor and stood on the tow bar, my legs straddling the universal joint. The mower should have been disengaged, but it wasn't, and my pant leg got caught in the still-turning universal joint. I grabbed onto the back of the driver's seat and held on for dear life as the spinning universal pulled on my pants with such force that my leather belt snapped in two and my khaki pants were literally ripped off my body. A moment later, I was standing on the back of that tractor in my underwear, shaking like a leaf.

When Daddy saw my shredded pants wrapped around that universal joint, he said to me, "If your pants hadn't come off, you could have been killed. Now you keep those pants as a reminder to be more careful." I've kept the remnants of those pants in storage for nearly sixty years. When I looked at them recently, I shuddered at what might have happened had I not managed to hold on to that tractor seat.

Farm life was full of dangers: heavy equipment, razor-sharp cutting tools, horses and mules that could kill you with a kick, poisonous snakes, seasonal floods, and guns in the hands of sometimes-irrational humans. Daddy was always overly cautious about my safety; one might even say he was paranoid about my getting hurt. I was The Only Son. There was no other to carry on his legacy.

Daddy told me many times that everything he did—buying

Hazlett, building the horse barn, breeding Tennessee Walkers, expanding our land holdings—was to make the farm bigger and better so I would be overjoyed to dedicate my life to it and eventually take it over when he retired. As I approached college, my anxiety increased with every repetition of "I'm doing this all for you." I was feeling increasingly ambivalent about farming as my profession, and it was becoming clearer and clearer to me that everything Daddy did was for Daddy, not for me. He was simply driven to achieve, and would have done so whether or not I was there.

As busy as I was with school and extracurricular activities, my obsession with male genitalia never lessened. It was especially confusing and troubling as I began to go out with—and *make* out with—girls. I did not "go all the way" in high school, but the heavier petting sessions always left me turned on, or beyond turned on. Looking back from this somewhat more sexually enlightened era, I understand that I was a bi-curious teenager. At that time, however, I was programmed to think it was normal (good) for me to like girls, abnormal (bad) for me to like boys.

My father's other favorite speech to me, which he delivered on a semi-regular basis starting when I was fourteen and continuing into my college years, went something like this: "Remember to keep your pants zipped. If you get a woman pregnant, we could be ruined. It could take away all we have and destroy our reputation." More so in college, but beginning in high school, I blamed Daddy for my remaining a virgin and not having intercourse even when the woman I was with wanted to.

On a deeper level, I knew I wasn't driven like Daddy to be with a woman sexually. I was passionate about seeing men unclothed, and I dreamt of getting my hands on a man—not to penetrate him or to be penetrated, I was sure of that—but to hold him, to look at him, to be alone and naked with him.

When high school let out for the summer the year I turned sixteen, and the days were long and hot, I would go down to our swimming hole on Cypress Creek. I would stand up to my neck in the cool water, enjoying the tug of the lazy current, thinking about my life and wondering what I might be if not a farmer. I felt trapped, oppressed by the sense that it wasn't the life I wanted, yet I could see no way to do anything other than what my parents had planned for me.

One day I was standing in the creek, lost in thought, when directly upstream, an enormous water moccasin, an extremely poisonous snake, came slithering toward me on the surface of the water. I knew that moccasins strike at anything that moves, so I held my breath and froze, not daring even to blink as the great snake slid past me, so close that the tiny ripples of his wake lapped my cheek. When I was certain he was well past, I staggered out of the creek, horrified, and never swam alone again.

But still longing for that cool midday immersion, I began going down to the creek when the colored farm hands would gather at the swimming hole for their lunch-time dip. I wasn't really with them, but I was there. They were so accustomed to me as a part of the farm, that they were barely inhibited by my presence, though I'm sure they refrained from gossiping about my parents when I was in their midst.

The cool creek provided relief and cleansing from their sweaty, dusty labors, especially during the time of the oat harvest, when the dust and chaff could drive you wild with itching. I would be in the creek upstream from them as they stripped off their clothes, bathed, dove, and relaxed, conversing in a vernacular so different from my own that I often couldn't understand what they were saying, though I always got the gist. Most of the men were in their late teens or early twenties; their work-hardened bodies were lean and beautifully muscled. I might tell myself I was less interested in them because they were black, but there was no denying they excited me.

So one blistering hot day during the oat season, I was standing up to my neck in the creek, watching the young men taking their lunch-time ease, when a flurry of excitement and laughter announced a contest among them. They were making themselves hard to see who had the largest wand. One of the men ran to the truck that transported them to and from the fields to fetch a yardstick.

The measuring device proved unnecessary for determining the grand prizewinner because a man named Lee was so prodigiously endowed. Seeing that extraordinary version of the object of my desire, I made a silent vow to get my hands on it as soon as possible.

Not many days later, I saw Lee going to the barn to feed the mules. I followed him, and when he climbed the stairs to the hayloft, I went up with him, my boldness a marvel to me to this day. We chatted briefly, looking at each other with mutual curiosity, and when I said I wanted to see him naked, he didn't act the least bit surprised.

Was I fearful of being caught with him in some forbidden act? Not at all. So tantalizing and mesmerizing was the prospect of being with him, it never occurred to me that his experience with me, whatever it turned out to be, would soon be the stuff of widespread gossip among the farm hands, though fortunately for me that gossip never reached white ears.

I remember the sunlight slanting through the cracks between the boards, illuminating the dust suspended in the breathless air. I remember my heart pounding, Lee standing before me in his overalls, so relaxed in his body and seemingly fearless. I asked him to take off his clothes; a moment later he stood before me, a brown Adonis, fully erect.

I gasped and said, "You are *so* big."

"Yessuh," he said gently. "I so big Lucille (his fiancée) can't take me yet. We put off the weddin' until she slep' around some and get more loose for me."

I undressed, too, and touched him all over, until finally I took hold of what I'd been longing to hold. We lay down in the loose hay together, but we did not have intercourse—there was never any question of that. I pleasured him with my hands and then satisfied myself against his hard body. I was never with Lee again; in a few months he married, and then left the farm to join the army.

My obsession was not quelled by this experience, but amplified, and I longed to touch a white man as I had touched Lee. This desire apparently communicated itself to a young man in our congregation. One Sunday evening after church, he invited himself to spend the night at our house. I assumed we might masturbate together, but he came to my bed in the middle of the night intent on getting into me. When I made it clear I had no interest in that sort of sex, he was miffed. He had assumed I was queer, when, in fact, I did not know *what* I was.

So the two great conflicts of my life continued unabated. My sexual confusion, characterized by that inner voice asking over and over again, "What's wrong with me?" ran side by side with my growing doubt about being a farmer. Yet I had no vision of what I might be instead. In the absence of a passion for another vocation, I could not bring myself to break my father's heart.

Whenever I tried to imagine myself doing something other than what my parents wanted, I would panic. Where would I go if I left the farm? How would I survive? My fear of the unknown was far stronger than my desire to go my own way, so I accepted my parents' plans for me and focused on the advantages of that seemingly safer course of action.

18
To Be or Not to Be

During my last two years of high school I was as busy as I've ever been in my life. If I wasn't starring in a play, cheerleading, taking part in speech competitions, or dancing and socializing, I was pouring energy into FFA (Future Farmers of America) projects. I raised steers, groomed and trained them, and won first place in competitions all over southwest Georgia. My steers not only topped 900 pounds with smooth layers of "finish," but were also "fitted" to yield prime-grade beef—always selling for top dollar per pound.

I was an excellent showman, too, which definitely gave me an edge over the more timid contestants. I almost always took first place in these contests, and there was often bitter talk among the losers that I had an unfair advantage because I started out with the best animals from my father's incomparable herd. It was true I got my pick of the litter, as it were, but it takes more than a good calf to make a champion.

I raised six to eight steers at a time. My steers would be auctioned immediately following the competition; I always made in excess of a dollar per pound, most of my steers weighing nearly half a ton. Making good money was a big incentive, as was the desire to please my father and mother.

The biggest money I made in high school came from a project that consumed much of my senior year. I rented fifty acres of new ground from my father. The stumps of recently harvested pines were still in the ground and I did not remove them. I broke the ground with an old-fashioned, mule-pulled plow, did half the plowing myself, and hired a man to do the rest. Then, I grew peanuts using the very latest techniques for planting, fertilizing, and cultivation.

Daddy was somewhat skeptical about my techniques, cautioning that I was planting my seeds too close together. My crop, however, turned out to be an historic one: I was the first farmer in that region of the South to achieve a yield of a ton per acre. The crop came to over fifty tons of peanuts, and news of my success was reported in the *Mitchell County Liberal*. With the proceeds, I paid off my rent to my father, covered all expenses, bought 125 acres, and still had money left over to put aside for college. Daddy then leased my land from me and farmed it while I was at the university.

My success with steers and peanuts apparently aroused the ire of an editor at the *Greenville Herald,* another paper in which my exploits were frequently reported. After I set the record for peanut yield, I went on to win Champion and Reserve Champion for my steers at the prestigious Valdosta Show. These accomplishments inspired a *Herald* article complaining that Jody Dixon was born with a silver spoon in his mouth, hired help did all his work for him, and *that* was how he was able to win all those prizes and awards. I have subsequently viewed newspaper reporting with a somewhat skeptical eye.

Mother was furious when the article appeared. She drove to Greenville, charged into the offending editor's office, gave him what for, and demanded a retraction. She told him that she and her husband and son worked hard to accomplish what they did, and she wasn't going to stand for such insults. Daddy and I were embarrassed by Mother's outburst. Daddy's philosophy was "Action speaks louder than words. Do the job well and ignore the petty fools who'd rather whine than work."

Speaking of the Valdosta Show, the prizes for Champion and Reserve were train trips to Kansas City via Nashville for a national convention of the FFA, paid for by Swift Meat Packers. When I was presented with *both* top awards at the show, I called the third-place winner up to the stage and gave him one of my trips. We had a great time on that little odyssey. I'll never forget our visit to The Grand Ole Opry where we saw Minnie Pearl and Little Jimmy Dickens. In those days the Opry was still being held in the original Maxwell House Opry Hall in downtown Nashville.

The last big event of my high school career was the senior class trip. All the town kids wanted to go to New York City, but several of the farm kids couldn't possibly have afforded such a trip. At the gathering to decide between New York and a bus tour of the Georgia coast, I spoke on behalf of us country kids. When the Georgia trip won out, my town friends snubbed me for a while, but I felt better knowing that everybody would get to go instead of just the kids from wealthier families. I had quite a bit of influence over my peers, proof of this my being voted Most Popular and Most Likely To Succeed.

During our stay at the King and Prince Hotel on Saint Simon's Island—they put us four to a room in the less expensive wing—I was taking an afternoon nap when I awoke to sudden pain. The class bully was pounding on me, cursing me for siding with the country kids and thereby denying the class a trip to New York. I curled up into a ball and let him beat on me. I never told a soul about the assault because I was ashamed of myself for not fighting back.

Then came the question of where I would go to college. At that time, America's finest animal-husbandry program was at Oklahoma A&M. It was Daddy's idea that I apply there, since the dean of the animal-husbandry school was a good friend of his. Daddy arranged for the dean to personally interview me, but then a few days before we were to make the long trip to Oklahoma, Daddy announced that he wasn't coming with me because he was too busy with farm work. As if that last-minute desertion weren't disappointing enough, the day before Mother and I were to leave for Oklahoma, I suffered a truly bizarre injury.

Daddy's prize Tennessee walking horse was a big beautiful bay stallion named Judge, his name written in lovely calligraphy over his stall. I had been out riding Jimmy, an easygoing gelding, and as I approached the horse barn, Judge came charging out to attack Jimmy. Judge had no intention of biting *me*, but as Jimmy shied away from his attacker, Judge sunk his teeth into the fleshy part of my leg. I bled profusely and was taken to the doctor.

For the next two days, as Mother drove those hundreds of miles to Oklahoma, I lay in the back of the car, weak and dizzy and in a great deal of pain. When I appeared in the dean's office, exhausted and disoriented, the dean was obviously chagrined that my renowned father hadn't deigned to come along. Instead, here was this woozy young man being presented by his overly aggressive mother. In the dean's eyes, I must have appeared to be the quintessential mama's boy. The interview was brief and tense; I left with the impression that my father's absence had predetermined the negative outcome. The dean was, of course, politic in his dismissal of me, saying, "Given your youth and the distance from your home, I think it would be more appropriate for you to come here to earn your master's degree."

That meant I would be going to the University of Georgia and majoring, of course, in agriculture. The University of Georgia main campus was five long hours away from the confines of home, and I *really* wanted to put some distance between my parents and me.

Which brings me to one of the more profound experiences of my young life. My Aunt Sally was married to Daddy's oldest brother Frederick. They lived about a mile from the home place. Aunt Sally was something of a loner and not well liked by most of the Dixon clan because she was very frank and never hesitated to speak her mind. I liked her very much and always felt comfortable with her.

One day I dropped in for a visit. I told Aunt Sally I had been accepted to the University of Georgia and that I was going to be an Ag major. She shook her head and said firmly, "Jody, you're not a farmer. You'll never be a farmer. It's not natural for you."

Her words stunned me because they were exactly what I'd been secretly thinking and feeling for so much of my life.

"By the time you're thirty," she went on, "you won't be farming. You'll be doing something completely different."

All I could muster was "Yes, ma'am."

I was roiled up by her prediction for a few days, but then I put it with all the other thoughts and feelings I was forever stuffing deep inside. Yet on my thirtieth birthday, thirteen years later, her words came back to me and I marveled at her foresight. In retrospect, I believe Aunt Sally must have had insight into the question of my sexual identity as well, and I wonder what she would have predicted about that.

19
The Great Escape

Having attended a three-year high school program, I was only seventeen when I entered the University of Georgia. I was not only younger than most of the other freshmen, but had also led a relatively sheltered life and came from a very small high school. Furthermore, a large number of the undergraduate males were World War II veterans attending college on the GI Bill. Many of my classmates had been in combat. So I began my college career feeling very much like a boy among men.

Being young was only one of the preliminary obstacles I had to overcome. Because of a shortage of dorm rooms for freshmen, my parents arranged for me to board with friends of theirs who rented rooms in their house, which was a good distance from the campus. Mother drove me to Athens—a long five hours—and got me settled in my room. When it became clear that Mother intended to stay around for several days to oversee every step of my new life, I promptly broke out in a hideous rash of red spots all over my face. Only in retrospect do I associate the rash with my mother's presence; at the time, I was too stressed to make a conscious connection between her hanging around and my physical distress.

The medically prescribed treatment for my rash was a bright green ointment to be daubed on the myriad spots. Therefore, when I joined the long line of freshmen registering for classes, I appeared to be afflicted with a case of green chickenpox. I was humiliated and so certain that no fraternity would offer to pledge

The Great Escape

a green-pimpled freshman that I didn't sign up for Rush Week until my sophomore year.

I entered college as the recipient of the one scholarship the College of Agriculture awarded to the outstanding entering freshman. The $500 prize did not endear me to my peers, but engendered the same kind of jealousy that had dogged my accomplishments throughout high school. Ironically, I had not applied for the scholarship; my high school FFA advisor had done so on my behalf.

So college began. My first roommate, a veteran in his early twenties, was an affable guy from Greenville. There was some comfort in his being from my neck of the woods and we got on well together in our room, which was furnished with a bunk bed. Two other men lived upstairs with us, older veterans, each with a small room; we four shared one little bathroom. Given my particular obsession and their veteran lack of shyness, I was thrilled to have daily views of naked men casually bathing and shaving.

One of the men was an amputee, however, his leg missing below the knee. I never felt comfortable seeing him undressed, with or without his prosthesis. He was one of the first deeply bitter men I'd ever known and I found his dark moods particularly intimidating.

In the course of that year I had sexual encounters with two of my three housemates. These were not sordid exchanges, but merely involved my gently pleasuring them with my hand. I wanted to satisfy my curiosity about how big they could be, and I wanted to please them. It was always very important to me that the men I pleasured in my relatively innocent way be pleased. If they wished to return the favor, which neither of these men did, all the better, but it wasn't something I demanded. One time with each, that was all; the experiences put no damper on our relaxed friendly relationships. I now realize that however unenlightened those times may seem now, there was an unspoken understanding among men who had been to war that sexual arousal among men was not proof of homosexuality, but an expression of innate urges transcending sexual preference.

My roommate was a Catholic, which was only significant because I had never met a Catholic or a Jew until I entered college. I had never lived anywhere but the home place, and had never been out from under the watchful eyes of my parents. For the first time in my life, most of what I chose to do with my time and energy was up to me. True, I was an Ag major because Daddy expected me to be, and that *did* determine many of the courses I took, but I no longer felt inclined to cram my days full of extracurricular activities or strive to be the top of my class. It soon dawned on me that I had burnt myself out in high school trying to be Super Achiever.

And what did I love to do more than most anything? Dance. So I went to all the dances I could possibly go to. The Big Band era was in full swing, and the University of Georgia was a regular stop for many of the best-known bands. Along with more casual dances that took place throughout the year, there were gala fall and spring dances featuring a famous big band on a Friday night, and that same band giving a morning concert the next day.

The Charleston was making a comeback, and I was determined to master that infectious style of dance. I watched the best dancers and memorized their moves, practicing in front of a mirror until I felt capable of dancing in public with a partner.

Even as a freshman I was fairly bold about asking women out, and all my dates were good dancers. There was many a night when my partner and I would be jitterbugging or doing the Charleston with a big circle of admirers gathered around, cheering us on. This kind of adulation did my self-esteem a world of good and gave college life a shine that even the drudgery of animal husbandry couldn't dim.

The Great Escape

I wasn't a great student, but I enjoyed college, and I *loved* living away from my parents. I sometimes think that had I been free of their expectations, I would have been a drama major, with a minor in architecture, or maybe the other way around. I had always loved architecture. To this day, my doodles are designs for houses and buildings, though I have no idea where this passion originated. In any case, it was not a fascination I felt free to indulge in college.

That first year was definitely a period of adjustment for me. As my freshman year drew to a close, I returned to college from spring break in possession of my mother's car. I had complained of the hassle of getting to classes on time, so Mother loaned me her almost new, dark blue Mercury four-door for the last six weeks of the semester.

Summer break came, and I was back at the home place where the familiar feelings and patterns began to reassert themselves, though they couldn't completely reclaim me now that I had tasted freedom. Knowing what it felt like to be left to my own devices, farm life held even less appeal for me than ever. I reveled as always in family reunions, hung out with my high school chums, and looked forward eagerly to my second year of college.

While Daddy was busy with his ever-expanding cattle and farming operations, my main job that summer was to spend eight to ten hours a day in the saddle, riding the pastures, counting the cattle, and checking them for disease and injury. I found the work mind-numbing, so to amuse myself I decided to learn to smoke cigarettes.

I would get a pack of unfiltered Camels from the store, ride away from the home place, and light up. My goal was to eventually be able to smoke a pack a day, but I never could get through more than one cigarette per hour, and whenever I tried to actually inhale, I would get so dizzy I was in danger of falling off my horse. After a few miserable weeks, I said to myself, "This is stupid," and threw the pack away.

That was the summer before Leah entered high school, and Dana was a rambunctious four-year-old. Mother was quite busy with them, but that didn't keep her from resuming her extreme watchfulness over me. When she tried to use me as her go-between with Daddy, I refused to play the role. The first time she said, "Jody, go tell your daddy I'm—"

"No," I interrupted her. "I'm not doing that for you anymore. You got along fine without me, so I'm not gonna do that." In the annals of teen rebellion that may not seem like much, but it was the first time in my life I ever openly bucked my mother. I believe it surprised her as much as it gratified me.

Not being their intermediary for those first nine months at college had caused an emotional revolution in me. I suddenly had much more energy for myself, and for the first time in my life I had privacy, *emotional* privacy, which I was determined to preserve.

The second year of college was a whole new experience because I lived in a dorm on the main campus, which made going to and from classes a breeze. The Agricultural College was on a separate campus about a fifteen-minute walk from where I lived, but my studies didn't focus there until my junior and senior years. I took basic agricultural classes during my first two years—poultry husbandry, cattle, swine, biology, and chemistry—and found most of those subjects unspeakably dull.

For my first quarter on campus I shared a dorm room with a law student who did most of his studying at the library. Though I rarely saw him, I'm fairly certain he didn't bathe for that entire quarter; still, his body odor was nothing compared to the more odoriferous sectors of the agricultural college.

I, by contrast, may have been the cleanest student on campus. Why? Because I showered long and often, having discovered that the dorm shower room was a vast tiled enclosure without

The Great Escape

separate stalls, where the parade of unblushing male humanity provided a constant source of fascination and inspiration.

I had a lovely little ritual for going to sleep. My favorite radio show, *Dancing in the Dark*, began at eleven every night. I would change into my pajamas, do a little dancing in front of the mirror, and then climb into bed.

I moved to another room for the last two quarters of my sophomore year. My new roommate turned out to be the polar opposite of my nearly invisible roomy of the first quarter. Patrick was a twenty-five-year-old veteran, a barrel of laughs, and had come to college with one primary goal: to play. Drinking and whoring consumed his weekends, and I enjoyed his company so much I often acted as his driver in various misadventures. By a stroke of luck, Patrick was also one of the few undergraduates who didn't smoke, so our room was spared the oppressive atmosphere that dominated college life in those days.

I was in possession of my own car for my sophomore year—a gift from Daddy—a Mercury convertible. For the purposes of chauffeuring Patrick to and from his favorite brothel, however, I drove his battered old Buick. I certainly didn't want to sit in *my* car down by the river on that dirt road in front of the whorehouse. And sit is what I did most of the time, while Patrick was inside, waiting to be his sweetheart's last trick of the evening.

Almost every night my sophomore year I would sup at The Varsity—the closest thing to a fast-food joint in those days—on the edge of campus. I ate the same thing every time: a chili dog and NIPC (No Ice Plain Chocolate) milk. By the time I got back to the dorm room, Patrick would be drunk and getting drunker. Then I would drive him down to the river where the two legal whorehouses in Athens stood side by side. Patrick was a devotee of Madam Bessie's, the rambling one-story house—rambling because of the several extra bedrooms added onto the back. He would make himself comfortable in the commodious living room and wait for his "girlfriend," Millie, to emerge from her room and give him the sign that he would be her last visitor of the evening.

Patrick encouraged me to join in the fun, and I did go in one time and observe the goings on for half an hour or so. But I was not tempted to spend the five dollars they charged to go all the way with one or another of the lovely young things who so aggressively offered themselves to me, so I returned to Patrick's car to await the completion of his escapade.

I did, however, stick around long enough to meet the love of Patrick's life, a pretty young woman with a tired, worn face, and a sadly sweet smile. Patrick desperately wanted to marry Millie, and had only kind words for her. One night, driving home from Madame Bessie's, Patrick told me that Millie had slept with *thirty* men before him that day. "But," he said with utter sincerity, "she saved her best for me."

Why did I accompany Patrick, and spend so many nights of my eighteenth year sitting in his car, waiting to drive him home? I enjoyed partaking of the bawdy, somewhat illicit drama of those nights. I was intrigued by the phenomenon of men paying for sex with women—the straightforward fulfillment of sexual need. But, I realize now, I was also hoping to absorb some of that essential, unadulterated heterosexual energy from Patrick, to become more masculine, more interested in sex with women. I also used those uninterrupted hours of silence to meditate on the mysteries of my life, to ponder: What's wrong with me? Why am I so different from other men? What do I really want to be? What will become of me?

As for my own romantic adventures, for those first two years of college I was dating a girl from a prominent farm family who lived an hour or so from Joleda Farm. Her parents liked me and thought I was a good catch for their daughter. But she was physically cold and seemed strange to me. Our connection, from my point of view, was mostly for show.

One sultry summer night, I arrived for a date and was greeted at the door by my girlfriend's older sister. "Sis is sick tonight," she said, a gleam in her eye. "You'll have to do with me." Well, we never made it to the movie theater. We parked at a cemetery behind a black church and that farm girl was all over me, ready to do everything and anything I wanted to do. That we didn't go all the way is testimony to both my timidity and my underlying lack of sexual interest in women. But the events of that night did confirm the futility of my continuing a relationship with my girlfriend, with whom I had far less chemistry than I had with her randy sister.

Virginity intact, I returned to campus where I continued the various routines comprising my life there. One of those was ROTC, then mandatory for all male students the first two years of college. ROTC entailed a rifle drill every Tuesday morning from 8 to 9:50, and an hour-long lecture on military topics three times a week. I knew I'd be drafted after graduating, so it was my intention to continue ROTC for the duration of college and enter the military as an officer rather than a lowly private. I was also required to take physical education those first two years; not comfortable with physically combative games, I stuck to tennis and swimming.

I continued to have occasional furtive sexual interactions with young men—never more than mutual masturbation—but I felt growing pressure to subsume those tendencies and prepare for what I knew would be the only acceptable course for my life: marriage, children, and fulfilling my parents wishes—spoken and unspoken.

20
The Brotherhood

Going out for the fraternity rush in the spring of my sophomore year, I received bids from Alpha Gamma Rho and from Kappa Sigma. Alpha Gamma Rho was *the* agricultural fraternity, but since the last thing I wanted was to be surrounded day and night by Ag majors, I opted for the smaller, quieter, and to my mind classier, Kappa Sigma.

Though I didn't move into the Kappa Sigma house until my junior year, I was initiated into the fraternity shortly after pledging. The initiation process was harrowing. To this day I cannot see a raw oyster without remembering that night and feeling slightly sick to my stomach. There were four parts to the initiation I recall most vividly, the first part being what I refer to as trial by oyster.

I was made to kneel, my hands tied behind my back. A fraternity brother stood above me dangling a raw oyster soaked in castor oil attached to a string. I was told to put my head back and open my mouth. My tormentor then lowered the oyster down into my throat where the morsel stimulated my swallowing reflex. When the oyster had nearly disappeared down my gullet, it was yanked up and out of me, bringing me to the edge of vomiting. This sickening process was repeated several times.

We were then led blindfolded from the house and downtown to the grand old movie house where, with the permission of the owners, three of the initiators, each with a supply of raw eggs, climbed up a ladder and positioned themselves atop the marquee. Then, as passersby stopped to watch, our blindfolds were removed and we were made to stand below the marquee, hands still tied. The men on the marquee, about twelve feet above us, then cracked open their eggs and spilled the gooey contents down toward us. It was our duty to catch the raw eggs in our mouths and swallow them. If we failed to catch an egg, we were whacked hard on the butt with a wooden paddle.

But that was kid stuff compared to the grueling final test. Thinking of it, I shake my head in wonder at the cruel imaginations of not very imaginative people. At midnight, we were led into a room where the carpet had been rolled up and the floor covered with newspaper. We were told to strip naked, and then we watched in fascination as a great quantity of corn flakes was dumped onto the floor. We were then doused from head to toe with maple syrup and made to roll in the corn flakes. When we were thoroughly caked in the crunchy cereal, we were instructed to put our clothes back on.

Blindfolded again, each of us was driven to a separate remote location, some fifteen miles out in the country. Left alone in the pitch dark, having no clue where we were, we had to make our way back to town, our bodies sticky and itchy under our clothes, which were soon soaked with sweat. Add to this scenario the following detail: it was a Saturday night and the black people thereabouts were enjoying their traditional alcohol-driven celebrations. We were not, on the face of it, their friends, and though my fear of them may have been somewhat exaggerated, it was not unfounded. Every time a car full of boisterous country folk came along the road, I dove for cover. Also, every farm along the way was patrolled by vicious dogs whose main purpose in life was to attack strangers, which we all were, and easy to smell at that. I found a big whacking stick as soon as I could, and when I couldn't avoid the dogs, I had to fight them off with a vengeance or be torn to pieces.

I reached the outskirts of Athens at dawn, scraped, scratched, bruised, and filthy from diving into ditches, scrambling through brambles, and battling snarling curs. I was worn out, body and soul. When I finally reached the fraternity house, it was all I could do not to burst into tears. Deeply relieved to have made it back safely, I showered, changed into clean clothes, and ate the big breakfast they had waiting. From that moment on, I was in the club. The formal initiation ceremony that followed was anticlimactic, but knowing that all my brothers had survived the same ordeal created an instant bond among us, a sense of belonging that was no small thing for me.

Our housemother, Mrs. Lucy Black, was a lovely woman. A widow in her early fifties, she had tightly curled brown hair and a big, warm smile. She took to me right away as I did to her. She had a little office adjoining the kitchen and could usually be found there from just after breakfast until late in the afternoon. If there were house social functions in the evening, she made every effort to be present for those, too. Since I had been made social chairman shortly after pledging, Mrs. Black and I had reason to spend lots of time together, planning menus for parties and making lists of needed supplies. I'm sure I would have sought her out regardless of my role as chairman, because I very much enjoyed her company.

I moved into the fraternity house in my junior year and almost immediately came to the realization that I couldn't live there for long. I had no doubt about wanting to be a member of the fraternity, taking meals there and participating in the social events, but sleeping and studying there were nearly impossible. There were too many of us to call the accommodations spacious.

I did, however, enjoy the nearness of all those new and fascinating male bodies displayed with the unabashed openness of young veterans of war. Indeed, the handsome young man who slept in the bunk below me woke every morning with a grand erection, so I was almost always awake before him to have the pleasure of that vision to start my day. I never did sample his charms directly, but I certainly admired his ever-readiness.

One evening during the incessant game of Crazy Bridge, this same handsome young man announced his plans to have his way the next morning with the prettiest of our young maids. We were all in agreement that she had a marvelous body and a lovely way of moving, but we doubted he would be successful with her. He proposed to stay in bed until she came to change the sheets, at which point he would encourage her, he said, to join him in the sack. Well, I woke the next day, desiring to watch our resident lothario fulfill his boast. Instead, I had to hurry off to class.

That evening after supper, our hero performed a stirring monologue in which he recounted every detail of his successful seduction of the sweet young thing. He began by miming the throwing back of his sheets and surprising her with his nakedness, then followed with a reenactment of his button-by-button undressing of the willing lass. He climaxed his performance with a pitch-perfect imitation of her cries of delight as he took his triumphant time with her for much of the morning. Or so he said.

I wasn't alone in finding life in the fraternity house too tumultuous for sleep and study. A fellow sufferer among my frat brothers learned of a room for rent next door in the home of a Jewish family: a rabbi, his wife, and their four young children, with a fifth on the way. Our room was situated directly above the kitchen, and was heated by a vent in the floor that permitted air warmed by the oven and the stove to rise into our room. More than heated, however, the air was freighted with so much garlic that our clothes, hair, and skin smelled perpetually of it, no matter how often we bathed. The children of the house conspired to be every bit as loud, if not louder, than the boys at the fraternity house, and so once again I made it known that I was looking for a more peaceful place to rest my head.

Fortune smiled on me once again. Across the street from the fraternity house stood the lovely home of Mrs. Waterson, a charming widow in her early eighties. Her house was a miniature version of the frat house, with a single large bedroom and bathroom upstairs. She was a true Southern lady: graceful, gracious, and generous. She made the upstairs room available, free of charge, to a young man she found quiet and agreeable. The current recipient of her hospitality was a Norwegian art major and fraternity brother. He was soon to graduate and thought Mrs. Waterson would take a shine to me. He made the introduction, Mrs. Waterson found me sufficiently charming, and I lived in her quiet home for the rest of my junior year and all of my senior year. I merely had to stroll across the street to take meals and socialize with my fellow Kappa Sigmas; at night, undisturbed by my noisy brothers, I slept like a babe.

Mrs. Waterson had a wonderful sense of humor, and it was my ongoing pleasure to make her laugh. She also had a splendid backyard garden with more than fifty varieties of irises. In the spring it was a truly breathtaking vision. I would sit amidst those flowers and study, raising my head every now and then to fill myself anew with the wonder of them all.

I was apparently her last, great favorite among those to whom she leant her room. When she died the year after I left her, her sons invited me to her funeral and told me I could have anything I wanted in her house full of wonderful antiques. I satisfied myself with two of her cut-glass bowls, which I still have.

My peaceful life with Mrs. Waterson was often in shocking contrast to the goings-on across the street at the Kappa Sigma house. For instance, there were two young women, telephone operators, who rented rooms in a house just up the street. They were good-looking girls who liked to flirt with the young veterans who sat smoking and drinking on the front porch of the frat house. One evening when Mrs. Black was away, the girls did more than flirt; they joined the fellows on the porch, had a few drinks, and then offered to take on all comers in bed.

In no time at all they were installed in two adjoining beds upstairs, a long line of eager young men formed, and for hours on end the brothers took their turns with the willing girls. To me, it was an utterly bizarre scene. Though I watched and waited with the rest, I knew I would leave before my turn came. The women didn't do this for money, but for pleasure, it seemed. I remember sitting there, a great mob of us in the room where the sex was going on, some of us even sitting on the bed with the lovers, if one can call them that, others standing, watching, and waiting. At some point I slipped away, feeling more certain than ever that I was not like most other men.

I began to date more often in my junior year, and though I had my share of passionate petting sessions with some of my girlfriends, I kept my pants zipped, telling myself that I was heeding Daddy's warning. I also told myself that it would be admirable to be a virgin when I married my virgin bride, though in truth I didn't believe there was any great virtue in virginity. I found myself most attracted to those women I had little hope of winning; bright and beautiful, and obviously intent on the more sophisticated men who belonged to the most prestigious fraternities—men who would one day be lawyers and doctors and leaders of their communities.

I began to restrain myself more and more from succumbing to the temptation of pleasuring other men. I told myself that such hanky-panky was a dead end, a phase I needed to leave behind for the good of my future. That said, there were still occasions when the opportunities were simply too good to pass up, and so I would occasionally indulge my passion. After each encounter, I was haunted anew by the questions: Who am I? And what's wrong with me?

Granddaddy died during my junior year. Essentially bedridden for the last two years of his life, he was attended by Grandmother, a nurse, and their cook. During spring break, I went to visit him in his house in Greenville. As I started up the front steps, I heard the most beautiful singing—Granddaddy's strong tenor mixing with the pretty voices of the cook and the nurse. They were singing the hymns he had sung thousand of times as a leader in the Cottonwood Methodist church. I went into the living room and sat listening, tears in my eyes, receiving their song as a gift.

When they had finished, I went into Granddaddy's room and sat beside his bed and held his hand. The women left us alone and we chatted for a while. He had never told me he loved me, nor did he tell me so then, but I knew he did. Though he was dying, I could feel his robust spirit coming through. I'll never forget that. He was the father of my father, the founder of our legacy, and it was important to me to feel connected to him in a loving way.

The summer after my junior year, I returned home to find my father largely incapacitated by his murderous migraines. He had overseen the planting of 1500 acres of peanuts, but because of his weakened state he put me in charge of fertilizing and cultivating the vast crop, as well as organizing the harvest, which took place shortly after I returned to college for my senior year.

I had a run-in with my parents that summer, which brought up all the old feelings of being suffocated by my mother and abandoned by my father. One Saturday morning, I'd slept in, having being out late with friends. Daddy came to my room, obviously uneasy about his mission, and said, "Jody, I'm concerned about your drinking. I– I found this empty gin bottle in your car and I want you to promise me that as long as you're living under my roof, you'll take more care and not drive while you're drunk."

I knew perfectly well that Mother, not Daddy, had gone snooping around my car, and had put him up to this lecture. I wanted to argue, to protest that I was not much of a drinker, never had been, and that I felt betrayed by his playing the part of Mother's lackey. But I wasn't capable of confronting him, so I promised to be good, and we didn't mention the incident again. The situation infuriated me, yet I stuffed my feelings, as usual, adding more volatile fuel to that great volcano of anger and resentment that would explode now and then throughout my life—though never at my parents—and would not be fully released until fifty years later during therapy.

I had two dramatic experiences that summer—one comedic, one tragic—involving my six-year-old sister, Dana, that seem emblematic of my life at that time. I loved spending time with Dana, and I'm certain that my enjoyment of her, and the deep sense of responsibility I felt when I was in charge of her, enhanced my desire to one day have children of my own.

I was baby-sitting Dana one night, Mother, Daddy, and Leah having decided to spend the night in Greenville. I locked up the house and settled down to sleep in the guest room with Dana. Just as I was drifting off, I heard a noise upstairs. In the deep quiet of the night, I distinctly heard someone coming *very* slowly down the stairs. The hairs on the back of my neck stood on end and my heart began to pound. Clump. Long pause. Clump.

Terrified, I crept out of bed, got my shotgun and a flashlight, and tiptoed to the bottom of the stairs. It was eight steps up to the landing where a door separated the upper part of the house from the lower. Clump. Long pause. Clump. I stealthily climbed the stairs to the landing. Drenched in sweat, I aimed my gun at the doorway, ready to confront the dread intruder.

"Who is it? Who's there?" I asked huskily.

No reply.

I opened the door and raised my gun. Something very small squeaked plaintively. I shined my light on the landing and froze a field mouse in the act of rolling a pecan down the stairs. The brave college student did not shoot the tiny mouse, but returned to his bed, shaking like a leaf.

The other incident, if not for the intercession of angels, astonishing good luck, or both, would have been the greatest tragedy of my life. I was driving to Cottonwood to meet Mother. It was dusk and Dana was beside me, drowsing in the humid heat. The road to Cottonwood was straight, rising and falling over the gentle hills. Dana slumped down and fell asleep. I was driving fast, roaring along in Mother's almost new Mercury.

We shot over a rise at eighty-five miles an hour, and there in front of us was a tractor-drawn wagon full of white sharecroppers—men, women, and children with their peanut poles—heading home after a long day's work. I hit my brakes, which sent Dana tumbling off the seat, but there was no way for me to stop in time or go around their wagon because of an oncoming car in the other lane, and a cement culvert on the shoulder to our right. So I plowed into the back of that wagon, the impact sending people and peanut poles flying in every direction. Two of the big poles struck our windshield; one shattered the glass in front of me but went no farther. The other penetrated the windshield and impaled itself in the seat back. Had Dana not fallen off the seat, the pole would have gone right through her.

Miraculously, only one of those people in the wagon suffered a broken bone; everyone else was merely bruised, scraped, and badly shaken up. The very next day, at Daddy's calm insistence, our insurance agent visited those people, members of two poor families, and paid the lot of them $5000 to sign releases exonerating me. And that was that—certainly a far cry from what would have happened today. Daddy acted in his usual swift and efficient way to protect me, and therefore the farm, from any claim that might threaten our future.

Back at college for my senior year, I barely won an alternative position on the prestigious livestock-judging team, but membership came into conflict with ROTC. Forced to choose between them, and seeing no way but to choose livestock judging, I had to drop out of ROTC. This was a bitter pill to swallow because I had essentially wasted three long years faithfully attending ROTC classes and drills. Even more galling was that I had attended boot camp at Fort Benning during the summer between my sophomore and junior years, a hellish six-week ordeal, my fallen arches put to the severest of tests, my feet and legs swollen and aching every night.

Ever the dutiful son, I swallowed my disappointment and applied myself to the judging team, knowing it would look good on my résumé and be a plus in what I thought would be my inevitable career in animal husbandry. I made mention earlier of my aversion to goat meat, goat cheese, and oysters. I will now add lamb and mutton to that list, and tell you why.

Judging a sheep, lamb, ewe, or ram, is far more complicated than merely looking at the animal. The body must be felt all over, obscured as it is by all that wool. To do this, a judge must stand over the sheep, bend down, and work his or her fingers under the wool and loose skin to determine the conformation (true shape) of the body and to assess the layers of fat. To develop this skill, team members had to spend a good deal of time in the agricultural college barn where the sheep spent the winter living in their own manure and urine, of which they stunk. After spending hours at a stretch delving under the filthy hair of these captive animals, no amount of scrubbing can remove that singular odor from one's fingers. To this day, that wretched odor returns to me whenever I smell or taste lamb.

Food, as you may have gathered, was of great importance to me. One of the great thrills of college life was being introduced to foods I'd never tried before. I had fried shrimp for the first time, and tasted my first lobster tail.

I also began experimenting with cooking for myself. Using Mrs. Waterson's kitchen, and Pearl's kitchen at home, I found that I loved the process of following a recipe as well as trying to recreate the flavor of some new dish I'd enjoyed at a restaurant or party. I discovered a love for arranging flowers, too, and began growing my own during summers at the home place.

In my quiet way, I took advantage of the relative freedom of college to open to my feminine nature, though I wouldn't have known to call it that. I *did* know that my time in college was fast coming to a close, and that military service would follow, after which would come the life my parents had designed for me, whether I wanted it or not.

21
Flying

I celebrated my twentieth birthday in the midst of an all-too-brief escapade that began shortly after Christmas of my junior year. Learning to fly was, without a doubt, one of the most adventurous and independent undertakings of my life. Had my love affair with flying lasted just a few hours longer, there's no telling what I might have done in life.

I was curious about the little Piper Cubs that flew over the campus, and one Sunday, driving around for the simple pleasure of exploring, I saw a little airplane rising into the sky and decided to find the airstrip. I parked where I had a good view of the grassy field, thrilling to each takeoff and landing. I began to imagine myself at the controls of one of those machines, and found myself longing to fly. I wanted to rise above the earth where I might escape the gravity of what other people wanted me to do.

So I went into the office and inquired about lessons. When they told me that each one-hour lesson cost only five dollars, I immediately signed up. There were no forms to fill out and no parental permission required, and so I didn't tell my parents until I had several lessons under my belt and knew it was something I wanted to keep doing. Aside from my car, which was a gift from Daddy, I paid for my entire college education with my own money. This was very important to me, and kept me from being too hard on myself about my lack of enthusiasm for many of my classes. Given a choice, I would have preferred almost anything to sitting in a stuffy classroom, listening to someone drone on about egg production in Iowa. I no longer felt driven to excel.

The Piper Cub, circa 1949, was a tiny single-engine plane, its fuselage and wings covered with remarkably thin canvas. The plane was extremely lightweight; it was no great chore for a single person to tow it along the ground. The Cub's maximum load: two people. By today's standards it was not capable of great speed. Pressed to go beyond 120 miles per hour, the delicate hull would begin to shudder—a most unnerving sensation.

My instructor was an air force veteran in his mid-thirties, a calm and patient man, very matter-of-fact about what was still a relatively new sensation for most of us—taking wing like a bird, albeit a noisy one. The engine was so loud that it was impossible to hold a conversation during flight, but the instructor was expert at communicating with hand signals. Once we landed, he would carefully review everything we had just practiced.

I went on my first solo flight after ten lessons. I took off, flew for a few miles around the airstrip, and then landed. Exhilarated by this accomplishment, I decided to increase from one weekly lesson to three. I felt free as a bird when I was flying solo; in fact, one of my favorite things to do for my hour in the sky was to chase buzzards. These huge birds fly fairly low, three or four hundred feet off the ground, and I had the confidence of the young; I never felt I was doing anything dangerous as I swooped through the air chasing those big black wings.

My other favorite thing to do was to follow the river course, flying low over the sparkling water, leaning into the curves as I flew. I was so happy up there, so open to all the feelings and ideas I kept bottled up on the ground, that for the first time in my life I began to have a sense of the mystic nature of reality. With no precedent for it in my intellectual development, never having heard about it from my parents, teachers, or friends, I began to envision myself reincarnating as an eagle; a spirit in the body of a great bird, spending my days drifting above the earth, all seeing, all knowing.

After seventeen lessons, my instructor and I undertook my first cross-country flight. This was in preparation for the solo cross-country flights I would have to make to get my license, which I was very eager to do. By then, my parents knew of my flying lessons and we decided to make the home place the destination for our cross-country jaunt, a distance of about 125 miles as the crow flies. The flight was delayed for a day because of rain, so we left on a Sunday morning instead of Saturday.

The weather was clear when we took off, and I was so excited I had trouble paying attention to the details of flying for the first fifteen minutes. I was flying home to show my parents that I could do something they'd never envisioned for me, something bold and adventurous. We flew by compass at about 5000 feet elevation, having marked our route on the map. I was preoccupied with spotting our landmarks, which detracted a little from my enjoyment of the trip, but didn't lessen my excitement. We approached the commercial airport in Greenville to refuel, and the instructor had me radio the tower to clear us for landing.

Once we had landed, I felt more at ease, and thoroughly enjoyed the last leg of our flight to the farm.

We landed on the front pasture, a relatively smooth, grassy field because it had previously been cultivated. Then we had lunch with my family. Mother and my sisters were thrilled, of course, but I was most gratified by Daddy's reaction. He was impressed and enthusiastic. He hinted at buying a plane for me to fly on business for the farm, and continued this kind of talk in several phone conversations leading up to my first solo cross-country flight.

I flew five more short solo flights around Athens, and then the big day arrived in early May when I took off alone for Greenville, the home place my destination once again. I hadn't slept much the night before the flight, and was anxious about the possibility of rain, the sky full of clouds. Because of doubts about the weather, I didn't take off until after lunch, which meant I would be somewhat pressed to arrive at the farm before dark. I was also nervous about communicating with the tower at the Greenville airport, not having the instructor along to make sure I said the right things. I was tense for much of that flight, making sure to identify places along the way, notably Ashville, Georgia, where I could make emergency landings if necessary.

Despite my fears, the flight went well. I landed and refueled in Greenville without a hitch, and had a great takeoff as I headed for the home place, where I arrived at twilight. To my dismay, I found the pasture where I was to land full of cattle, Daddy nowhere in sight. I had called ahead from a pay phone at Greenville, and Daddy had assured me that all would be ready when I arrived, but that was clearly not the case. I buzzed the field three times, swooping low over the cattle in hopes of scaring them away, but they wouldn't budge. Finally, in the thickening dusk, Daddy arrived with several farm hands to drive the cattle to one side of the pasture, leaving the center clear for landing.

Now came a trickier part of the adventure. I would be coming in from the south, which meant I had to slip down over a stand of tall trees, a somewhat difficult maneuver that required me to pull back on the throttle after clearing the trees so the plane would drop, and then throttling up to give me enough forward momentum to land without hitting the ground too hard. Since I was already going slow, the drop I made after clearing the trees felt very much like falling, but I executed the slip perfectly and landed without mishap. I emerged from the plane to find my somewhat subdued father, exhilarated mother, and about twenty-five farm hands.

But the ordeal was not yet over. Here came all these curious Herefords with their sharp horns, eager to inspect the mysterious thing that had landed in their pasture. The vulnerable fabric covering the plane could easily be torn by one of these unpredictable beasts, and the plane had to be protected from that. So as darkness fell, we dragged the plane to one corner of the fenced pasture where, in the light cast by the headlights of several farm trucks, Daddy oversaw the hasty erection of a barbed-wire enclosure. He kept berating himself for not clearing the field of cattle, and I could tell from the tone of his voice that his enthusiasm about my flying had waned considerably. I told myself it was a passing mood and that he would soon regain his fervor.

Over supper, Mother said she was dying to have me take her up for a flight so she could see the farm from the air. Daddy wanted nothing to do with such adventures and even tried to talk Mother out of flying with me, but she would not be deterred. In the morning over breakfast, as Pearl prepared my snack for my flight back to Athens, Daddy was very quiet. I recognized his silence as a sign of anxiety over my safety.

Mother enjoyed her flight immensely, praised me to the skies, and encouraged Daddy to go up with me for an aerial view of his domain. He merely shook his head and asked me to call him the minute I landed in Athens. I took off from the home place at ten that morning—a perfect takeoff—and, the weather fine, flew to Greenville to gas up again. I had a stellar, anxiety-free flight back to Athens, and even chased a buzzard along the way to celebrate. I landed with ease and was congratulated by my instructor who said, "Now you only have nine more hours of cross-country solo to get your license."

I hurried to the pay phone and called Daddy, but before I could even begin to express my elation, he blurted, "I was scared to death worrying about you crashing. Now I want you to promise me that as long as you're living under my roof you'll never fly again. I want you to promise me you'll quit."

And I heard myself answering, "Yes, Daddy. I promise."

That was not, however, quite the end of my romance with flying. I still held out hope that after I turned twenty-one and graduated from college, Daddy would relent and I would get my license and fly my own plane around the country on farm business. This hope, however illusory, softened my disappointment and allowed me to return to the more mundane concerns of college without feeling too depressed. As I had so many times, I stuffed my feelings of disappointment and abandonment deep inside, and then carried on.

The finale of my love affair with flying came the next year. My birthday, March 21, fell during spring break, and I had never missed celebrating that day with my parents and sisters. But for spring break of my senior year, I was invited to go with three good friends to a fishing camp near Capps, Florida, for a few days and nights of relaxation. These were fraternity brothers my own age, none of us veterans, and my going with them meant that I would celebrate my twenty-first birthday with my buddies, in a rustic little cabin on an isolated stretch of river, before bringing them to the farm the next day for a party with my family.

I had a wonderful time fishing and resting, while my friends had a good time drinking. At supper on my birthday, they presented me with a cupcake with a candle in it, to which they sang a boisterous version of Happy Birthday. I felt grownup and independent, and went to sleep that night smiling about the feast I knew awaited us at the home place.

A three-hour drive brought us to the farm. Mother, who was uncharacteristically subdued, had a big meal waiting, and in my honor she served it on her good china. Daddy too was subdued, and I knew something was wrong when neither of them greeted me with "Happy Birthday." When the meal ended, I naturally expected a birthday cake to appear, but none did, nor was my birthday ever mentioned. My friends all gave me glances that meant, "What's going on, Jody?" Then, as we were getting ready to depart, my father called me aside and furtively handed me a check for $500. "This is a graduation present, in advance," he murmured, "and a little something for your birthday, too."

That was that. I felt sick to my stomach all the way back to Athens. I'd had visions of a joyful celebration, of Daddy announcing he was going to buy a plane for the farm, of receiving a special present or two, and feeling my parents' love for me, however timid and guarded. But they didn't have the generosity of spirit to celebrate my coming of age, or to congratulate me on being me. At the time, I made the assumption that they treated me as they did that day—humiliating me in front of my friends—because Mother was miffed about my not being there on the *actual* day of my birth. I'm sure that part of why she denied me a cake was to punish me for choosing *anything* over her, but the deeper truth was that this was yet another concerted action to discipline me, to train me to conform to their wishes. No independence for Jody. No airplane. No flying. No separate life. And once again, I bowed to their combined will.

Decades later, the events of my twenty-first birthday welled up during a group therapy session. After experiencing again that terrible feeling of being crushed and abandoned, I began to release powerful bursts of suppressed anger. Then, at the height of my rage, my therapist said, "What would you like to say to your mother, Jody?"

Propelled by an enormous upsurge of rage, I jumped to my feet and flung an imaginary glass of iced tea in my vividly imagined Mother's face. "Take that, you bitch!" I cried.

"What about your father?"

"You coward!" I bellowed, seeing him lurking in the shadows. "Why didn't you stand up to her?"

22
Mother's Shame

The summer after my senior year, I made a firm decision to direct my energies to finding the woman I would marry. To complete the picture of myself as a whole, competent man, I would require a wife and a family, just as my father and grandfather had. To further this process, I enrolled for an additional quarter at the University of Georgia, taking the relevant business courses to complete my qualifications for overseeing a large, multifaceted commercial farm.

I banished my attraction to men to the nether regions of my conscious mind, and set out wholeheartedly to find the future Mrs. Dixon. It is barely an exaggeration to say that I eventually dated nearly every eligible young woman of good reputation living within a hundred miles of Joleda Farm.

My father was not content to farm thousands of acres of peanuts and cotton, and to raise Tennessee walkers and great herds of registered Herefords. Two years before I graduated from college, he added registered hogs to the list of livestock offered by Joleda. He renovated the shed on the side of the horse barn to accommodate his latest: red Duroc and black-and-white-spotted Poland China hogs to sell to other breeders. He announced this enterprise to me with the usual "I'm doing this all for you" speech, though I no longer believed him.

I made no outward protest, but thought, *Hogs? Who wants to fool with stinkin' hogs?* After all, one of my childhood chores involved the mongrel hogs we kept in the pecan orchard. It was my job to keep their watering trough full and the ground around the trough wet so they'd have a wallow. I remember hurrying away from the hogs at dusk, racing down the little footpath through the dry grass, wanting to get home before dark for fear of stepping on a rattlesnake—a fear I inherited from my father.

Despite my misgivings about tending to Daddy's purebred hogs, I dutifully delivered litters of pigs, often in the middle of the night, for the next two summers and for the year after college. I would set my alarm for 2 A.M. and go down to the farrowing shed to check on the pregnant sows. It was essential for a human to be present at the birth of the piglets, otherwise the sow might roll over and crush some of the newborns. Every piglet was money in the bank; we didn't want to lose any to carelessness. Our record litter was fifteen little porkers.

As I had silently predicted, the stench from the operations became unbearable, and Mother insisted that Daddy build a new hog barn a quarter mile from the house. Ever the zealous builder, he erected a state-of-the-art facility with air conditioners suspended over the two farrowing stalls. Being the inventive man he was, Daddy ran a flexible hose from the air conditioners down to the sows so they could have cool air blowing on their noses while they were in labor. He also hired a swine manager when he realized that I was not eager to assume that position.

With every passing day, it became clearer that Daddy was incapable of sharing power with me. One day during that first summer after I graduated from college, he sent me to oversee the building of several hundred feet of wire fence. Having done it many times before, I knew how to build fences, and this was a simple job. I was nearly twenty-two and perfectly capable of directing the four men assigned to work with me.

Nevertheless, Daddy accompanied us to the site, gave the initial directions, and then left us, only to return two hours later.

He visited twice that morning and twice more in the afternoon to make sure we were fulfilling his precise expectations. The reality of my future clarified itself that day in the following realization: Daddy will give me responsibility, but no real authority. Being an entirely self-made man, it was not part of his makeup to relinquish control of anything important to him.

That night I lay awake absorbing the significance of this. I saw that a clash of wills or a parting of ways was inevitable. I didn't voice my concern to anyone, but from that moment my search for a wife became invested with a conscious desire to get out from under the control of my father and mother.

Meanwhile, I refused to give up some of the habits I had developed in college, notably the cooking and eating of fine food, served in a fine atmosphere. I would commandeer the kitchen and prepare lobster tail, a baked potato, and sautéed vegetables as I had experienced them in the restaurants of Athens and Atlanta. Then I would eat supper by candlelight, alone on the porch at a little card table set with linen cloth and napkins and our best china. Mother frowned upon what she took to be my growing eccentricity. "Jody," she would say, glaring at me in her imperious way, "why do you want to go to all that trouble? There's food in the fridge. I'll put some in the oven for you."

As I sat there in the soft glow of the candles, eating the delicacies I had come to love, I felt keenly how different I was from my parents. This was no longer about sexual preference, but about my cultural aspirations. Four years at the University of Georgia had enlarged my vision of what was possible; I craved a richer, fuller life than was available on the farm. This further amplified my desire to find a way off *their* path and onto one of my own choosing.

So I completed an extra quarter of classes in Athens and returned home at Christmas with no plan other than to work for Daddy until the army called me. In January I was invited to judge a local Hereford show in Kennesaw. I'd been asked to judge because I had been on the judging team in college *and* because I was the son of Harvey Dixon. Tickled by the honor, I drove up for the show and stayed overnight in a motel, feeling very mature and accomplished. Though there were only thirty entries in the show, I gave it my all.

On my way home, my head began to ache. By the time I reached the home place I was in excruciating pain. When I got to the doctor in Cottonwood the next day, I was beginning to experience intense itching and pain in my scrotum. The doctor thought I might have pneumonia and admitted me to his twelve-bed hospital. He started me on a course of penicillin—the new magic bullet—but it did nothing. Along with a soaring fever, my scrotum became ulcerous and swelled to the size of a grapefruit. Baffled, the doctors took samples of the pus from the ulcers and sent them to Atlanta for examination. My temperature rose to 105 degrees and hovered there for days on end, no matter what was done to reduce it.

I truly thought I was going to die. I begged Daddy to take me to a hospital in Atlanta, where I knew the medical care was more advanced, but he said, "No. You'll have better care here because everyone knows you."

So I languished for several more days in a feverish delirium; my temperature peaked at 106 and then slowly began to drop. After two weeks in the clinic, the report came from Atlanta: I had Rocky Mountain Spotted Tick fever. I spent another four weeks there, and then Daddy and Mother took me home. I was too weak to walk and stayed in bed for *another* six weeks. My doctor wrote to the draft board and I was excused from conscription until May. Slowly but surely I recovered. The tick must have been in the hay bale I sat on between rounds of judging those Herefords in Kennesaw. As ticks will do, it found refuge in the moist warmth of my crotch and feasted on my blood.

Mother's Shame

My brief reprieve from military service turned out to be the window of opportunity through which I would meet my future bride, though our initial meeting would pale next to a tragic drama that befell our family that very day.

I had only been back on my feet for a week or so when I accompanied Daddy to a big production Hereford sale at a prestigious ranch in Thomaston, fifty miles from the home place. A production sale means that the cattle were raised there. This was a neighborly appearance on Daddy's part—one prestigious rancher visiting another—with a courtesy purchase, however nominal, expected of Daddy. The ranch was one of three owned by Mr. Paterson, his principal business being the sale of automobiles in Lexington, Kentucky. At this sale I caught my first glimpse of my bride to be, though we weren't introduced on that day.

Mother came to the sale in a separate car, having first dropped my sisters at school, and she left the sale ahead of us to return home. Not long after she had gone, Daddy was called to the phone. The coroner in Tripoli, about twelve miles away, was calling to say that Mother was in trouble and we should get there as soon as possible. Hastening to Tripoli, we found Mother in a stupor of shock and grief. While driving through the little town in our big new Chrysler, she had been unable to stop in time to avoid hitting a six-year-old boy who had darted out from behind a bush into the road in front of her. He was killed instantly, struck first by the hood ornament and then with the following mass of the car.

The coroner's inquest was held on the spot and the child's death declared accidental. I was given the job of driving the bloody Chrysler home, where I parked it behind the store to spare Mother the sight of it. Then I took it upon myself to wash the blood off the hood ornament and front bumper. Daddy sold the Chrysler back to the dealer in Cottonwood the next day.

Mother sat in shock and misery for the next three days,

attended by women friends from the church. On the day of the boy's funeral, Mother came out of her stupor and said, "I have to tell his parents I'm sorry." She had Daddy drive her to Tripoli where she tried to present a bouquet of flowers to the boy's mother. The grief-stricken woman screamed at Mother in rage and grief, and slammed the door in her face, which sent Mother into an even deeper depression.

Not long after that, the dead boy's parents sued Mother for damages; when a settlement could not be reached, a trial date was set. Mother refused to drive for several weeks after the accident. When she did resume driving she would only take the dirt road to Cottonwood, driving slowly and parking on the outskirts from where she would walk into town rather than risk driving down streets where children played. She considered herself a murderer. She was not only ashamed of herself, but also deeply embarrassed. Mother was a perfectionist about all things external; killing that little boy was, to her, a horrible blemish on her reputation.

I too was in a state of shock for weeks after the accident. Having so recently been in an accident of my own, when the peanut pole might have killed Dana, I had great empathy for Mother. I prayed that she would come to accept the child's death as an accident, but she never could. Thereafter, she became much more reclusive, though still deeply involved in the lives of her daughters. Daddy was supportive of her, but they had never been emotionally close, and the accident did not draw them closer.

23
Tying the Knot

When Daddy held a production sale of Herefords—barely a month after the death of the little boy—Mr. and Mrs. Paterson returned the favor of attending our sale, bringing their daughter with them. The first time Esther saw me, I was standing ankle deep in manure, showing off a promising young heifer. I was interested in Esther the moment we were introduced. She was five feet eight inches to my five-ten, with dark brown hair and big, beautiful blue eyes behind her glasses. She was blooming with health, well groomed, and had class. Well educated, soft-spoken, and somewhat reserved, she chose her words carefully and evidenced no vanity about having lived such an advantaged life. In short, she was a real lady, and a devout Christian to boot.

When Esther and her mother came up to the house to use the bathroom, I waited for them on the porch to ask Esther for a date. Having known her for only a few minutes, I already had the feeling she might be the partner I'd been looking for. I liked her, and was very impressed by her parents. Since I intended to have children, my wife's parents would be the grandparents of our children, and I wanted them to be exceptional people. Esther's parents were intelligent, sophisticated, successful, and Christian. Marriage was serious business to me; blind passion played no part in it.

Esther seemed mildly pleased by my interest in her and said I might come visit her at their Thomaston ranch before she returned to Lexington, Kentucky, where she lived with her parents and worked as her father's personal assistant. We had five dates in that one week, which meant I drove 110 roundtrip miles five times, and though I was more certain after each date that Esther was "The One," she never let things go beyond holding hands.

I liked her caution and reserve, qualities that only fueled my determination to woo her. She was warm and friendly, and wonderfully easy to be with. I loved making her laugh and she seemed to love that I could. There was something inexpressibly delightful about being so comfortable with each other, and I think that emboldened us to take things further.

She informed me that she had no intention of ever marrying, having been jilted some years before by a seminary student she'd expected to wed. But she also admitted that she'd come to the sale at Joleda because her father had noticed me at his Thomaston sale and told her, "The Dixons have a son, and he looks like somebody you should know." Since she worshipped her father, she came; I saw, and was now hoping to conquer.

On our fourth date, Esther said to me, as if it were a revelation of deep, dark significance, "You know, I'm older than you are."

"I thought you might be," I said, loving the sound of her voice. She spoke with a clear, resonant timbre, having been a contralto soloist with her church choir.

"*Lots* older," she said gravely.

To which I replied, "Unless you're over forty, I don't care."

That made her laugh. She was twenty-five and I was twenty-two. By then I was certain she would be a good mother to her children, which made her all the more attractive to me. In retrospect, I realize that part of my drive to win her sprang from a desire to create the kind of family I had longed for as a child — with a warm and loving mother *and* a loving father at its helm.

Tying the Knot

As our fifth date drew to a close, still without even a friendly hug from her, I approached Esther with that intention. She straight-armed me at the door and said, "If you're ever in Lexington, come on by and we'll give you a home-cooked meal." I laughed uproariously as I drove away, excited by the challenge of courting her.

I waited a day before calling her in Lexington. I had yet to tell her I was going into the army, because I didn't want that to influence her feelings about me. I told her I wanted to come see her, and when she gave me permission to come, I detected a note of excitement in her voice. So I drove the 600 miles to Lexington, and stopped at her father's auto dealership to get directions to their farm. One of Mr. Paterson's minions told me that Esther was at a church meeting and wouldn't be home for some time.

I drove out to their farm and was staggered by the size and beauty of the place, which was kept as fastidiously as my father kept Joleda. Their main house resembled Mount Vernon. Too intimidated to wait alone for her at such an imposing mansion, I parked at the show barn, feeling more comfy with the cows and whiling away the time talking to the farm manager. When Esther pulled up in front of the main house, I could tell by the sparkle in her eyes and the eager way she got out of her car that she was thrilled I'd come to see her.

My anxiety disappeared the moment I was in her presence; I was so comfortable with her, and we were so relaxed and natural with each other, that I forgot all about being intimidated. She and her parents were just as genuine and friendly toward me as they had ever been, inviting me to stay for a few days.

I took Esther to dinner that night. When I brought her home, I kissed her for the first time. Little did I know how appropriate it was that our first kiss was in a car. That kiss broke the ice and I felt emboldened to tell her that I was going into the army in a few days. She wondered why I hadn't told her before, but she seemed impressed that I hadn't wanted impending military service to influence her feelings for me. I then spent a day getting to know her father by attending a cattle sale with him in Paris, Kentucky; I could tell he liked me and approved of me for his daughter.

On a sparkling spring afternoon, Esther and I drove out onto a beautiful hill on her father's land; she told me this was where she planned to build a house and raise the two children she was going to adopt. It was almost unheard of in those days for an unmarried person to be allowed to adopt children, but her father was well connected politically and was a major contributor to a Baptist children's home, so there would be little trouble arranging things for her.

She told me again that she had no intention of ever marrying. I think she saw herself as a kind of secular nun, but I was determined we were going to have children of our own together. I just happened to have brought along the architectural plans for my own dream home. I got them out and said, "How about something like this?" I was nothing if not bold.

I think she was both baffled and impressed by my ambition regarding her, which no doubt reminded her of her father's way of wrestling with life. We were both extremely interested in discussing the pros and cons of our potential union. Our genuine feelings for each other were overlaid with mutual pragmatism, Esther being even more analytical in her thinking than I.

What seemed a few heartbeats later, I was in the army, which both removed me from the ongoing gloom overhanging Joleda and distanced me physically from Esther. While Mother continued to struggle with her despair about the boy's death and the dreaded trial, I began sixteen weeks of basic training at Fort Jackson, South Carolina, during which I was unable to get away to visit Esther. For the first two months of my enlistment, Esther was on a tour of Europe, culminating in her attending the coronation of Queen Elizabeth. Her perfumed letters made me the focus of attention at mail call, since the mail clerk could never resist making a show of sniffing Esther's letters before calling my name and presenting the scented envelopes to me.

I wrote to her whenever I had time, and after her return from Europe, I called her every Sunday using my father's phone card. I finally convinced her to come visit me, but being a virtuous, religious woman, she wouldn't come alone; she enlisted her brother to be our chaperone. I booked them an air-conditioned hotel suite—it was terribly hot in the summer there—and I sent her brother off to the movies so Esther and I could do our courting in private.

As my focus on wooing and winning Esther intensified, my infatuation with men retreated even further into my subconscious. I began to believe that whatever had been wrong with me had evaporated in the pure Christian heat of my desire to marry and raise a family with Esther. I wanted to be faithful to my wife and worthy of God's love, so I turned my thoughts wholly to loving her and no other.

As winter approached and the nights grew colder, I complained to Esther in a love letter that they left the barracks windows open and my feet were getting chilled at night. I wrote, "I long to sleep with you, sharing the warmth of our bodies."

"Buy a hot water bottle. It's cheaper," she wrote back. I howled with laughter when I read that, my confidence unshaken.

In October of that year, less than six months after meeting her, I got a weekend pass and drove home to Joleda with two engagement rings I'd bought in Atlanta, one traditional and one marquis. I mounted them atop a bottle of RSVP perfume and wrapped the package elegantly. The Patersons were in residence at their Thomaston farm, where I presented Esther with the package. When she opened it and saw the rings, she threw up her arms in fright, but I wasn't dismayed by her reaction. Two emotional hours later, she chose the traditional ring, as I guessed she would. We agreed on a six-month engagement to give us time to get to know each other better.

As it happened, our wedding took place only three months later, so her brother could attend the wedding before leaving for Alaska to serve as an officer in the air force. Esther and I were married in Lexington on a snowy winter day in 1954. There were over 1000 wedding guests at one of the largest Baptist congregations in Kentucky, of which Esther's father was the leading light. Esther and I were both glad and relieved not to have to wait another three months before tying the knot. We had discovered that we truly loved each other, emotionally and physically, and were absolutely convinced that it was God's will that had brought us together.

Esther told me before we married that the only reason she went out with me in the first place was because her father encouraged her to consider me as a potential partner. This is not to diminish how much we loved each other, but it is one of several aspects of our marriage that was not particularly romantic or passionate. We were, in our own humble way, aristocrats of an emerging South; it was a relief for both of us to know that we were social equals, religiously compatible, had the approval of our parents, *and* that we enjoyed each other's physical presence. Indeed, our first year of marriage, full of the unexpected adjustments newlyweds have to make, was made much easier by the sensual and sexual pleasures we shared.

Shortly after Esther and I were married, the day of my mother's trial finally arrived. The whole bloody mess was about to be relived again before a jury, the judge ready to take his seat, when a deal was struck between the two sides. Mother had survived twelve hellish months, but she was aged beyond her years by the ordeal.

Tying the Knot

Throughout that year, consumed by military service and courting Esther, I had maintained a close attachment to my parents. I hadn't yet replaced the vision of working for my father and living at Joleda with a new vision of the future. Indeed, plans were underway for us to build a house on my father's land as soon as I had served my two years in the army. But I had not reckoned on the dynamic intercession of a man with power and ambition that dwarfed those of my parents—Esther's father.

24
Bouncing Around

One of the basic rules for increasing one's chances of survival in the military is Never Volunteer, a rule I broke after only a few weeks in the army. We had just completed a grueling sixteen-mile hike over hill and dale; my feet were absolutely killing me. When the powers that be announced they were looking for someone who could type, I raised my hand. Never mind that I had earned an "Incomplete" in typing in high school. I became a company clerk, and most of my South Carolina hiking days were over.

Shortly after Esther joined me at Fort Jackson, I bumped into a fraternity brother who was also stationed there. He was getting ready to give up his civilian component duty as a doctor's driver. With the recommendation of my fraternity brother, I got the job, a sixty-five-dollar-a-month raise, *and* was freed from the confines of the clerk's office. The nature of the job, however, brought me face to face with the sexual obsession I had so recently suppressed in favor of heterosexual love.

My chauffeuring of the good doctor, Captain Chekhov, involved picking him up at his home and taking him to the base's main physical exam station. From there, several times a day, I shuttled blood samples over to the lab for him. But most of the time I just sat in that examining station, watching an endless parade of naked young men, many of them beautifully endowed. I tried not to gawk, but I *did* gawk, and my mind was full of all this at the end of every day when I would return home to my bride. Our sex life certainly didn't suffer from these daily viewings, and I was reassured that in the absence of such temptations I would soon stop thinking about men in that way.

Speaking of temptations, Esther fed me so well and bounteously in those first months of marriage that I gained twenty pounds. Remembering those first married meals always puts me in mind of the Friday treat of our newlywed lives. We'd buy matinee-priced tickets before six o'clock, and then go to the famous S&W Cafeteria, where I almost always partook of their ninety-nine-cent dinner special: turkey with dressing and all the fixings. Then we'd saunter back to the cinema and lose ourselves in the magic of the big screen.

Our sixteen months together in the army would be the last stretch of time Esther and I would spend as just the two of us. When Esther took my hand and placed it on her tummy, and I felt our baby move inside her for the first time, I wept for joy at the miracle of life. I felt so grateful to be united with Esther and to be making a family with her.

Before the baby was born, having spent several weekends going with Esther to Joleda, my grave misgivings about our living and working with my parents surfaced anew. I was now certain that Daddy would never allow me to move into a commanding position on the farm until he was too enfeebled to continue, and it was also clear that Mother and Esther were not natural allies. I doubt that Mother would have approved of *any*one I married.

Nevertheless, three months into Esther's pregnancy, there we all six stood—Daddy and Mother, Mr. and Mrs. Paterson, Esther and I—in the pecan orchard at Joleda, surveying the site of the house Daddy was going to build for us. I felt sick at heart because I knew that building a house on Daddy's land would be such a finality, a fifty-ton ball and chain that would tie us there irrevocably. I felt sure that such a move would be a disaster for us.

Perhaps my father sensed my ambivalence; shortly after this uneasy gathering, Daddy decided it would be a good idea for me to go to Lexington and work for Esther's father in his Ford dealership to learn the ropes of sales and public relations. His new vision of me was as the PR man for Joleda Farm. Thus we would not collide. In his inimitable, self-assured way, Daddy described how I would travel the country, wowing potential buyers and quadrupling sales. He was certain that Esther's father would be open to my coming to Lexington, and I realize now that my charismatic father-in-law had probably made the offer to my father before it was presented to me.

We took up residence in a small farmhouse on the Paterson estate in Lexington and waited happily for the birth of our first child. But the baby was in no hurry to come out and I was compelled to return to Fort Jackson on May 1. To make it possible for me to be on hand for the birth, labor was induced on April 30. The very next day I said goodbye to my wife and new baby in the hospital and raced back to Fort Jackson.

Upon my discharge, however, I didn't return immediately to Lexington, much to my wife's everlasting chagrin. Instead, I went to Joleda at the request of my mother. The psychic cable connecting us was still in place, her power over me unbroken. Using her most plaintive tone, she implored me to come to her the minute I was free of the army, "Because once you're settled in Lexington, I might not see you again for *two years*."

I came to realize what a disloyal mistake I made in not putting Esther and our newborn before my mother. At that moment, however, I was simply overwhelmed by the events of my life. In a poignant way it makes a kind of sad sense that I would go home to my parents at the end of one momentous phase and the beginning of another. I wish I had gone to Esther instead, but there is no undoing the past.

So I went to work at Paterson Buick, one of my father-in-law's smaller dealerships, and found that I was good at selling cars. Esther and I began in earnest to fix up the little farmhouse—long abandoned before we moved in — and settled into the routines of marriage and parenthood.

Mr. Paterson obviously liked me, and appreciated my work ethic, directness, and ambition, which was akin to his. I could tell he was gratified that he had chosen me as his son-in-law, and was happy that I had spared his daughter a lonely spinsterhood.

In conversations with Daddy and Mother, it was still assumed that I would eventually return to Joleda Farm; the sales skills I was acquiring would benefit my career as a rancher and farmer. But once again, the course of my life would be determined by my powerful overseers and not through any conscious action of my own.

Whether Esther's father and Daddy conspired to initiate what next befell us, I cannot say, but in retrospect it appears they were in concert. Though I was enjoying my new life as a salesman, Esther's father made us an offer we simply could not refuse. So Esther and I "bought" the Paterson farm in Thomaston, with a new house and 1000 highly improved acres, just fifty miles from Joleda. Daddy gave us 250 head — one quarter of his breeding stock — as a startup herd, and made it clear to me that he considered us partners with him in the cattle business. Backed by our fathers, two of the most prominent ranchers in the South, we were virtually assured of success.

After four months, however, riding a horse several hours every day to check my cattle, I was bored out of my mind and longing for more business activity, more excitement, more society. Esther, on the other hand, seemed content with our new life. She was committed first and foremost to our marriage and raising our children. She did not push me to make a change, but when her father invited me to join him for his annual visit to Detroit to schmooze with the automotive bigwigs, I couldn't wait to go. I'd been wracking my brains for something to make life more interesting; I even considered opening a car dealership in Thomaston. I had a great farm manager, but the ranching life was not for me.

When I came back from that trip to Detroit and tried to resume the ranching routine, I was miserable. I suffered through two more months until one morning, as I was riding my horse, it came to me clear as a bell: "I need to be in Lexington with the master." I had worked with Esther's father long enough to know that he was the man I wanted to learn from.

That evening, with no warning to Esther, I called her father and asked him, "Do you need another salesman at Paterson Buick?"

He replied with obvious pleasure, "Yes."

"I'm ready to come," I said. "Now."

Esther sat up, shocked, and said, "I did not influence you. This was *your* decision."

I was happy to take responsibility for the decision, because it was *mine*, not Daddy's, not Mother's, not the army's. *I* was deciding what to do with my life, and it reminded me of how it felt when I decided to take flying lessons. I was following my intuition, and it felt *so* right.

I drove to Joleda the next day and told Daddy we were selling the farm and moving to Lexington. He never said one negative word about my decision. He took back his cattle, and even helped spread the word that our farm was for sale. Though she didn't say so, I think Mother was secretly pleased that I was forsaking my father's game plan and choosing a more urbane ambition. At a greater distance, she could idealize me more easily and begin sending me love letters—written expression of her desire to be entangled with me.

As Esther and I were awaiting the movers, a man arrived at our door. "I hear your farm is for sale," he said eagerly. "I want to buy it." I showed him around the place. Three hours later we made the deal for $25,000 *more* than the note I'd signed for the farm six months earlier. Esther and I took this as a sign from God that we were making the right decision to change careers and move to Lexington. Talk about a whirlwind! But the greatest gust of all was soon to follow.

Arriving in Lexington, we moved into a little house we'd bought for $20,000, and I went down to the Buick dealership to get to work. I was met there by my father-in-law, his accountant, and his attorney. They had a contract for me to sign, stipulating that I was to be the *president* of the company. I was completely overwhelmed, having imagined myself starting at the bottom as a salesman and working my way up.

Overwhelmed or not, I rose to the occasion. When I was introduced to the fifty employees of the dealership, I made the following acceptance speech: "I know you all love Esther, and now you have a family member here full-time to work with you. I can't be your manager without your support. You have experience, I have none. I still have cow manure between my toes." That got a laugh. "I'm available. My door is open. I expect you to be my teachers."

Esther too was overwhelmed by my sudden ascendancy; in later years she would declare that it had been a mistake—too much responsibility too soon after leaving our farm behind. But I didn't think it was too much. I wouldn't tire of responsibility for the next thirty-eight years.

So Aunt Sally's prediction came true. Long before I was thirty, I was out of farming. I was a city-dwelling businessman, an active Baptist, not a Methodist, a married man with a child and more on the way. As it happened, I didn't recall Aunt Sally's prediction *until* my thirtieth birthday—one of the most difficult of my life. On that day I felt a sense of dread about leaving my twenties—those grand and momentous years—and settling deeper into what appeared to be an ultra-traditional lifestyle, its patterns and promises virtually set in stone.

Prosperous, happily married, a father, a deacon in the Baptist church, supported by a large community and extended family, I was well on my way up the ladder of success. I had long since ceased to hear that inner voice asking, "What's wrong with me?" So why did I experience a sense of foreboding?

I think that in remembering Aunt Sally's prediction, I also remembered how she really *saw* me, saw beyond the pretense of my painful effort to conform to what others expected of me. A true psychic, she saw the real me. And so, feeling the undertow of predictability taking hold of me as I turned thirty, I may have opened to the idea, if only for a moment, that I was still not free of pretense, not yet in full possession of my truest self.

25
Angels of Death

As we waited excitedly for the birth of our second child, I became a zealous Baptist in the church of my in-laws. Though we were a big-city congregation of several thousand souls, our order was not liberal. Even dancing was considered sinful. Heaven forbid! Since we were both non-drinkers, Esther and I didn't join a country club, a decision I now regret. Contact with a non-religious social group would have broadened our social base and given our children a much wider spectrum of experience. Instead, the church was our sole society; I threw myself into that community with great energy and dedication. Our congregation was, in many ways, that big family I had longed for all my life.

In short order I became a deacon and close friends with the pastor and others of high standing in the congregation. There were those who resented my sudden ascendancy to a privileged place in their midst, but I ignored this envy, having so often experienced the same sort of enmity before. I was happy to belong, and happy to give myself to my new community. I've never been one to feel guilty about my good fortune; I must credit my parents and grandparents for being exemplars of creating one's own destiny through positive intention and strenuous effort.

Our newlywed lives were busy and quite stressful for me. Six months after settling in Lexington, I experienced the first of the debilitating migraines that would besiege me for the next twenty years. And I encountered another troubling item: my explosive temper. In the subservient roles I played in childhood and young adulthood, I had always repressed my anger, but as the boss of a large company and the head of a fast-growing family, I found it impossible to completely suppress. I managed to control it at work and in business dealings, but at home my anger would erupt, often grossly out of proportion to whatever the triggering event happened to be. I was perplexed by these regrettable outbursts toward my wife and children, and it would be many years before I would uncover the deeper sources of my rage.

Every two years from 1955 until 1961, a child was born to us. I loved being a father, as Esther loved being a mother. In parenthood, she and I shared our deepest bond. Devoted to our children, we always made an effort to harmonize our care; wanting to be in agreement as often as possible when it came to raising them. I was determined to spare my kids the emotional trauma I had experienced as my parents' go-between and the object of their competition. By today's standards my hands-on care of our babies wouldn't be considered unusual, but in those days I was definitely a more nurturing father than most.

In 1961 our fourth child was born and we believed our family was complete. Esther and I had dreamed aloud together many times about having four children—two boys and two girls—and now we had them. I was a fully accredited car dealer, my business growing steadily, and had proven myself in the eyes of my in-laws. My father-in-law had obviously put his trust in me from the beginning, but my mother-in-law had had her doubts about me when I first joined their family. My devotion to her daughter and our children, along with my immersion in the society of our church, convinced her that I was a good egg. She and I eventually became quite close, and I counted her as one of my very best friends. All seemed to be well and our future looked bright indeed.

Then, in 1964, at the age of two and a half, Edward, our youngest, got the measles. When his illness did not run the usual

Angels of Death

course, we called the doctor. A few hours later we were on our way to the hospital. Our boy had contracted spinal meningitis and there was no cure for it. We were condemned to sit by his hospital bed watching helplessly as he convulsed and hemorrhaged internally, the hemorrhaging visible beneath his translucent skin. The doctor told us that if by some miracle Edward survived, he would be "a vegetable."

Esther and I could do nothing but stay beside our boy and pray as we witnessed the end of his life. We had not slept for two days and were both ill with fatigue and worry. A rollaway bed was brought into the room for Esther, who collapsed into sleep beside her dying child. I put a few pillows on the floor and lay down to rest while a nurse sat beside our convulsing baby and held his wrist to monitor his pulse.

Our pastor had been to visit us and we had been praying ceaselessly. At first my prayers had been for our child's survival, but before I fell asleep my prayers changed and I asked God to grant our son whatever would be best for him. I thanked God for the blessing of that little angel's presence in our lives for two and a half wonderful years. Shattered to the core, I prayed for his release from suffering.

I was awakened in the depths of that long night by a dramatic shift in the atmosphere. Something huge and powerful had entered the room. I sat up, and though I could see nothing in the dim light, I felt a presence I would thereafter call the angel of death. I was not frightened; on the contrary, I felt uplifted and filled with hope, as if a spirit from a dimension beyond this one—the realm to which our child's spirit was going—had awakened me.

As I sat in the presence of this blessed spirit, immersed in the amazing energy of Edward's release from this life, the nurse went to fetch the doctor, who arrived a few moments later with resuscitating equipment. Esther was roused and we were asked to leave the room. I knew intuitively that our son was gone, and though I would grieve mightily for years to come—never fully closing the wound of that loss—I did, in those moments of communion with that transcendent force, feel blessed by God.

The weeks following Edward's death were the most emotionally wrenching I have ever known. It felt terribly unnatural to me that my child should have preceded me into death. I vowed never again to allow myself to be hurt so deeply. I was terrified of experiencing such excruciating pain again. To this day, I am aware that I hold myself back from being as open, trusting, and loving as I was before the death of our little boy.

Esther's grief was unbearable, too, without the hope of new life. She wanted to get pregnant again as soon as possible, so we gave ourselves to passion amidst our grieving and made another baby. Esther was forty, which in those days was considered too old to be safely pregnant, but she was healthy, strong, and determined, and I was eager to do whatever might help relieve our sorrow.

Just three weeks before our fifth child was born, my mother had a stroke and died. She was fifty-nine, her death wholly unexpected. Sadly, I had become estranged from her the year prior to losing our son, and his death did not bring Mother closer to me. Two events stand out as the causes of our rift. The first was that, when Mother's mother died, our *eldest* son was in the hospital suffering from nephritis that had sprung from his bout with scarlet fever. I refused to leave him to attend my grandmother's funeral; Mother was furious with me for not rushing to be with her; she complained that this proved I didn't love her. Her dismissal of my son's grave illness as less important than a funeral infuriated me. The second event, far more distressing, had to do with my father being admitted to a private hospital because he had begun to experience blackouts.

Esther and our children and I were returning from a visit to

Esther's parents in Florida when we heard that Daddy was in a hospital in Atlanta. We came home via Atlanta and stopped to visit him. The doctor in charge of the case told me that my father's blackouts, which often followed murderous migraine headaches, were undoubtedly caused by the terrible strain between him and Mother. The psychiatrist recommended therapy for both of them, jointly and separately, but my mother refused to cooperate, saying flippantly, "There's nothing wrong with *me. He's* the weak one."

That tore it for me. Mother's unwillingness to help Daddy was more than I could stomach; I decided to minimize my contact with her from then on. At the time of her death, I was still so consumed with grief over the loss of our son, and so deeply involved in the impending birth of our new baby, that I didn't have the emotional wherewithal to properly mourn her passing. I found myself feeling more angry than sad about it; for all my ambivalent feelings about her, Mother was a smart, dynamic woman, and I was angry with God for denying my children the firsthand experience of their grandmother's dynamism.

This anger continued to bubble up for a year after Mother's death, until one morning, while driving to work, I recalled the prayer she'd so often made in my presence while I was growing up: "God, let me live until my children are educated. Let me never be a burden to anyone." I pulled over and allowed myself to weep, realizing that her prayers had been answered. She died shortly after her youngest child graduated from college, and because she did not linger in illness, she was no burden to any of us.

I was, of course, not yet healed of the psychic wounds connected to my mother, who was still rampant in my unconscious, and it would be years before I would enter intensive therapy, where I would confront the totality of her influence over me.

I think, too, that I experienced some relief when she died.

Throughout the years that I lived at a distance from her, beginning in college and continuing until her death, she wrote me long letters, essentially love letters. I became expert at skimming over the long passages of her praise and adoration and, yes, her longing for me, to find the bits of news and gossip that served to legitimize her romantic gush. As she had tried to possess me completely in my childhood, so, in these letters, did she idolize me.

Esther and I rejoiced when our fifth child—our third daughter—was born, and three years later our sixth, a son. Our doctor was upset with us for taking the risk of having a child when Esther was forty-three, but she was not to be deterred. The loss of Edward had lit a fire in both of us, to bring *two* souls into the world to replace the cherished one we'd lost. Now we had three girls and two boys, sweethearts all.

The birth of our sixth child was not the only great event at that time: Daddy remarried, and I take some credit for his dating and marrying one of the most loving people I've ever known. As it happened, I knew Margaret, a wonderful woman, recently widowed, from the Baptist congregation in Thomaston where I had been baptized. I spoke to Daddy on the phone one Sunday morning before church, told him that she was a prize among women, and suggested he call her.

Well, he called her that very afternoon, beginning their conversation by saying, "Jody suggested I give you a call." He took her for a drive and soon after they fell in love. Two and a half years after Mother's death, Daddy and Margaret began their twenty-nine-year marriage. She inundated my children with generous love, and they adored her in return.

My faith in good therapy is enormous, and much of it derives from the relief I experienced after reliving Edward's death thirty-five years after the fact in the presence of a skilled and compassionate therapist. The scars of that trauma will never completely disappear, but having now thoroughly expressed my anguish about losing him, I have full access to my happy memories of him and the joy he brought to my life.

My feelings surrounding Mother's death were much more complicated, and my grieving for Mother in therapy was entangled with all the other issues concerning my emotional enmeshment with her. Still, it was a relief to honor her death with all the deeply felt emotions and grief and gratitude that were inaccessible to me at the time of her dying.

26
Happy Chaos

Much like my father and grandfather before me, I began to lose my hair when I was still a relatively young man, and there were interesting consequences. One occurred when I was thirty-seven and we were moving to a new house across the road. I was giving our youngest girl her bottle when the movers arrived. I was nearly bald by then and quite overweight. The foreman of the movers entered the house, smiled at me feeding our baby girl, and said, "What a cute little granddaughter you have."

Offended that he thought I was so old, I replied somewhat nonsensically, "I'll have you know this is straight lineage." This event foreshadowed what happened eight years later when our youngest child started school. He announced to us that he was embarrassed to have such "old-looking parents" when all his schoolmates had such "young-looking parents." By then I was completely bald and Esther's hair was turning gray. Pressed by our son, I tried on a hairpiece in Miami. I enjoyed how it changed me, and said to Esther, "I'll wear a hairpiece if you'll color your hair." I thought no more of my vow until a few weeks later when I came home to find a beautiful brunette cooking supper. I got a hairpiece that was so expertly made and well fitted that only people who'd known me bald knew it wasn't my hair.

I couldn't resist premiering that new coiffure at church during our monthly business meeting. Ever the ham, I wanted to unveil my rug in a surprising way. Five hundred people were in attendance as I waited in the shadows of one of the church's huge supporting columns. When the pastor, who was balding and had taken to plastering his remnant strands across the bare expanse, called me to the pulpit to make my report, my emergence from the shadows aroused great murmuring and laughter. When I put my arm around the pastor and said, "So, which one has the Toni?" it brought the house down.

(If you don't get the joke, I must explain that there was a popular hair treatment for women in those days, heavily advertised on television, called Toni. In the ads, a depressed-looking young woman with lackluster hair stands next to her sister, a radiant woman with shining curls, the announcer intoning, "Which twin has the Toni?")

The pastor and I were good friends, so there was no danger of my offending him with my irrepressible humor. Early in his tenure as pastor, I went with him and several other church members on a hunting trip to the Big Horn Mountains in Wyoming. We stayed in a hunting lodge at 10,000 feet elevation, our quarry being elk. Though I wasn't really interested in hunting, I was in love with that wild country. One morning before dawn, I was dropped off at my stand to wait for an elk to come by so I could shoot him. No elk obliged me, but I did have a deeply spiritual experience.

At the first rays of sunlight, my spirit soared into an exultant state, and I sat there for hours, reflecting on the death of my son, of my mother, and of our previous pastor, recently deceased. I felt blessed beyond expression. The elements of spirit were showing me that life and death were inseparable.

Thoughts of death often followed me into my sleep in those days. Shortly after our last child was born, I started having a recurring dream that I was lying dead in an open coffin, yet I was conscious. Various people would file by, including my very best friends, and I would observe their faces. Never was a single tear shed for me. In therapy I returned to this dream several times because it was very disturbing. I came to understand it as metaphoric of my inability to reveal myself, my *real* self, to other people. The visible part of me in the dream is dead, while the unseen part of me is still alive, yet inaccessible even to those closest to me.

Inspired by this dream, I would employ a *real* coffin to good effect during a business slump in the 1970s. Sales were down, and it seemed that everyone at the dealership was sitting on their hands and allowing the tenor of the times to dampen their enthusiasm. I decided to shake things up. I had a casket on a rolling stand delivered to the hotel conference room where we'd scheduled a breakfast sales meeting. I placed a large mirror in the casket so that anyone looking inside would see his or her reflection. Then I closed the lid. My sales staff arrived and we had our meeting, everyone eyeing the casket with curiosity and concern. Then I opened the casket and said, "I want each of you to file by and look inside. I want you to tell yourself what you see, and then think about your sales performance." Half the staff was angry with me for putting them through this, and half seemed amused. In any case, sales *did* suddenly increase.

A natural showman, as was my father-in-law, I was forever dreaming up ways to grab the attention of the public to enhance my business. One of the greatest successes in my early years of running the dealership was a three-day sale we held at the state fairgrounds. This monumental undertaking involved renting one of the huge exhibition halls and moving all of our inventory and personnel from the dealership to the fairgrounds. The carnival atmosphere we created was infectious; sales were so brisk that customers literally raced each other to claim the cars they wanted.

My other brainstorm for that sale was to hire a gigantic crane to hoist an automobile forty feet in the air and hold it suspended over the parking lot outside the exhibition hall. This part of the fairgrounds happened to be right next to the beltway. I ordered the car hoisted into the air at 4 P.M., just as rush hour began. As you can imagine, the sight of that brand-new automobile dangling in the air caused traffic to back up for miles. When the police came looking for me to give the order to have the car lowered, I was nowhere to be found. That night, I watched with delight as the traffic jam and my dangling auto made the evening news.

My lifelong love of auctions, especially livestock auctions, took me to the state fair every year to see what the Future Farmers of America had to offer. One year I bid for and won the grand-champion steer and displayed him in the dealership showroom for three days. The presence of a live steer in our showroom garnered all sorts of free media coverage; then, I had the steer slaughtered and threw a huge party for all my employees and their families and friends. We barbecued that champion beef, along with several dozen chickens for those who had developed a personal attachment to the big steer and felt squeamish about eating their pal.

Another aspect of the automobile business I thoroughly enjoyed was taking things in trade; I would take almost anything in trade to make a sale. Of the many bizarre stories springing from my trading mania, one of the strangest had to do with a six-grave cemetery plot, valued at $297. I kept that plot on the books until its value had increased to $2000, then advertised the plot in the newspaper. A middle-aged couple expressed interest. The woman wanted to buy the plot, but the man did not, so we parted ways. Five days later, I received a call from the funeral director of that cemetery informing me that the man of this couple had suddenly dropped dead. His widow wanted to know if the plot was still available. Shortly thereafter I signed the deed over to her.

I attended many conventions and conferences connected to the automobile industry as a regular part of my business. Sometimes,

Esther would come with me. We were at a convention banquet in Greenbriar, West Virginia, when it was announced that there would be a dance contest, specifically the Charleston. Despite our church's edict against dancing, Esther enjoyed showing me off as a dancer when we were not in Lexington. She bragged about me to everyone at our table, and I was enthusiastically encouraged to get up and compete. I danced solo, stole the show, and won the trophy. Esther would never dance with me in Lexington, but when we were out of town she would humor me with a dance or two because she knew I loved it.

Our years of marriage were filled with travel; Daddy and Margaret funded many of our more grandiose adventures. In 1970, Daddy paid for my three eldest children and me to spend seventeen days in the British Isles. That was my first trip to Europe, and I was hooked.

Closer to home, Esther and I established a family tradition of renting a big houseboat on Lake Cumberland every summer when it was scorching hot; the best thing for the heat was frequent dips in a deep, cool lake.

Twice a year, we traveled to Joleda so the kids could spend time with the Dixon side of the family. We drove our station wagon, the drive taking twelve hours on two-lane country roads. Maribelle, our maid and nanny, accompanied us on these journeys, which we made in the late 1950s and throughout the '60s, when, despite the civil rights movement, segregation remained entrenched in much of the South. Because Maribelle was colored, she was not allowed to eat with us in restaurants, so we brought her food out to her in the car.

We needed to make three or four stops for gas en route, our policy being not to buy gas anywhere that didn't provide rest rooms for colored people. More often than not the answer would be "No colored." To which I would reply, "Then no buying gas."

As we continued on our way, our children asked, as they often did, "Why are they so mean to colored people?" I don't know that I ever answered that question to their satisfaction, but Esther and I always did our best to teach our children that all people are equal in the eyes of God.

In 1971 I won a trip to the islands of Greece, and Esther and I had one of our rare weeks away from the children. We liked getting away, just the two of us, on these occasional trips abroad. They recharged our marriage.

In 1973 Daddy decided to go to Australia to investigate ranch land he'd heard was selling for a dollar an acre. He took my eldest son and me along, as well as his farm manager and his bookkeeper. We had a great adventure, three generations of Dixon men traveling together. From Australia, we all went to Japan, except for Daddy, who changed his ticket and went to Perth. He caught up to us in Hawaii, where we were joined by Esther, the kids, and my sisters and their families. Daddy paid for the entire odyssey. I couldn't help but recall those early days when every little penny had mattered so much.

In midwinter of 1974 Daddy and Margaret flew to Geneva, Switzerland, rented a Mercedes, and drove all over that snowy country, looking for a chalet to rent for the coming summer. On the edge of Villars they found a place with awe-inspiring views of the Alps. Margaret's family stayed with them there for two weeks, while Daddy's children and grandchildren came for the other two weeks. Daddy brought along Eddie, his cook and house man at Joleda, to prepare our meals, and once again Daddy footed the bill for everything.

I took my job as a parent very seriously, as did Esther, and though I was busy with business and church duties, I made every effort to spend a good chunk of time alone with each of my children every week. My father had not been available to me when I was a boy, and I vowed not to repeat that pattern with my own children. I did, however, become much less spontaneous and carefree as the years passed, which I regret for my children's sake as well as mine. But life *was* serious: we had lost a child, and that colored our lives and the lives of our surviving children forever.

Daddy's murderous migraines had vanished when Mother died. I set out to cure myself of migraines, using a technique of my own invention. As far as I know, the process I developed came from no outside source. Once I committed myself to ending the twenty-year plague of migraines—*determined* commitment being the key—I began to study my situation carefully. My headaches would usually come on in late morning at work. If I left the workplace, the headache would eventually go away; if I stayed, it would linger. I deduced that something at work was causing the headaches, which might seem absurdly obvious, but when one is in the throes of a serious migraine, nothing is obvious.

I would pinpoint the igniting cause of the migraine—usually a conflict with an irate customer or employee. Once I knew the source, I would repeat aloud to myself, "I'm not going to let anyone else control my health and my mind." After six months of this practice, I no longer needed to leave my office to stop a headache from developing. I would simply close my eyes, relax, and repeat the affirmation of being in control of my own health until the threat had passed.

Curing those migraines gave me a new sense of inner strength that would serve me well the rest of my life—I could bring those same skills to bear on anything I wanted to accomplish.

In 1978 Daddy sold Joleda Farm, an event that literally ended an era of Dixon family history. Granddaddy's original fifty acres had been ours for nearly a century. At the time of the sale, Joleda covered over 5000 acres; my sisters and I were each given a quarter of the sizable proceeds. As a condition of the sale, Daddy retained the house and the surrounding five acres until his death, which made the emotional transition of giving up the farm much easier for all of us.

At Thanksgiving that year I asked Daddy, "How would you feel if I spent part of my Joleda money to take my family on a trip around the world?" Daddy was thrilled to know that his hard-earned money would once again be used to fund a journey of epic proportions.

In 1979 we circumnavigated the globe in forty days and forty nights, with only a half-day's rain along the way. We flew on twenty-three airplanes and stayed in eighteen hotels. We experienced not a single reservation screw-up, nor lost any baggage, and enjoyed the services of an excellent driver and a knowledgeable guide in every city.

No matter what country we visited, no matter how remote the locale, whenever it became known that we were from Kentucky, we were inevitably asked the same question: "Do you know Colonel Sanders?" When I replied that I not only knew him, but had also sold him a car, we were transformed from mere tourists into minor celebrities.

And so the first twenty years of my life in Lexington came to a close, headaches behind me, bald head covered with a realistic hairpiece, five children fast becoming adults, and business doing well. My wife and I were successfully navigating the river of a long-term marriage, and the loss of our son, though forever a sad memory, was no longer a daily sorrow. I had experienced powerful spiritual connections to God *outside* of church, and was looking forward to many more trips abroad. True, I was getting weary of the stress of the car business and hungering for a new challenge, something more creative, but I was not unhappy. Not consciously.

27
Trouble in Paradise

Upon our return to Lexington from our circumnavigation, I experienced a rare bout of depression. After a bit of soul searching, I admitted to myself that travel would not solve the problem of my waning interest in being a car dealer. Fortunately, my eldest son had proven himself an excellent car salesman and business manager, so I began the process of turning the day-to-day running of the dealership over to him. Thereafter, I devoted more and more time to what would become my next career: real estate development.

My inner voice had not asked "What's wrong with me?" in over twenty years, nor had I spent a conscious moment reflecting on my youthful obsession with naked men. Then in 1979, in my twenty-sixth year of marriage, I attended an auto-industry convention in Atlanta, where that age-old question was revived. I was sitting in the hotel lobby after supper, when a man about my age walked by and I experienced a full-body jolt of recognition. He sensed my reaction and turned to face me. I stood up and we gazed at each other with all-knowing eyes. A fraternity brother, he was one of the men with whom I'd had a sexual encounter in college.

"You staying here?" he asked, smiling slyly at me.

"Yes," I answered, feeling as if a rattlesnake had struck me.

"Let's have a drink and go to your room," he said with absolute confidence, as if certain of my response.

Visions of what we'd done together in our youth flooded into my mind and I stammered, "No, no. Not now. No. Not now."

He frowned curiously and then turned away, leaving me shaking violently. I hurried to my room, glancing over my shoulder in fear that he might follow me. In the privacy of my hotel room, my inner voice thundered, *What's wrong with me?* In a flash of clarity, I realized that I was *not* afraid of this man revealing my past and ruining my reputation. No, my fear was that I was still attracted to men, that men could arouse me, and that everything I'd worked so hard to establish—family, business, community—was threatened by the emergence of this long-suppressed "disorder."

At this same time in life, my dream of lying in a coffin was superseded by another recurring dream, one much more terrifying. *I am falling into a black abyss, hurtling down, arms and legs flailing desperately.* Then I'd wake up, heart pounding, frightened, and perplexed. My unconscious was talking to me, but I couldn't understand the message.

As I turned fifty, our youngest daughter entered therapy, which precipitated Esther's and my doing the same. I was anxious about it, but concern for my children's health always came first for me, and outweighed my misgivings. For a year and a half we were involved in both group and individual therapy. We discovered what we both had long suspected: Esther and I were focusing our energies on everything but each other; our communication had become largely pragmatic or superficial; we had stopped sharing our feelings; and along with this lessening of emotional sharing, we had become much less physically affectionate. Our therapist immediately recognized these signs of estrangement and focused on improving our communication skills, with much good resulting.

The other boon of therapy was that I made preliminary contact with my vast reserve of repressed anger and sorrow about my parents' emotional domination of me. I was not yet ready to go as deep as I would need to go to effect permanent healing, but it was a start and prepared me for further and more profound therapeutic experiences.

Having uncovered some of my feelings of abandonment by my father, I decided to make a conscious effort to be more physically affectionate with him and to tell him I loved him whenever comfortable opportunities arose. He had *never* shown me any physical affection, nor had he ever spoken those three little words—"I love you"—that I had always longed to hear from him. When we visited him, I began giving him hugs and made a point of telling him that I loved him whenever we ended a phone conversation. The effect of these simple gestures on my part was a profound blessing for all of us: Daddy became a hugging grandfather who said "I love you" to his grandchildren more and more often with each passing year. This taught me that even the most emotionally closed person has the potential to be set free by the example of expressed love.

For the next few years—the early 1980s—America was in a recession. During these tougher economic times, my son lifted much of the load of the dealership from my shoulders. Turning my attention to real estate, I made three major purchases: a

370-acre farm and estate on the western edge of Lexington that became our new home; a defunct planing mill and lumberyard on one and a half acres in what was becoming an upscale retail area in Lexington, and a three-bedroom apartment on the beach in the Cayman Islands, a Caribbean paradise.

In 1985, three of my children and I became certified scuba divers—one of my main motivations for buying a place in the Caymans. Learning to scuba dive at age fifty-five was the beginning of another of my life's great love affairs. My first instructed dive was a spiritual experience, the elation I experienced reminiscent of how I felt at nineteen, when I first took to the air in a Piper Cub.

I felt inseparable from the miracle of existence. I could feel myself changing and healing as I surrendered to the bliss of being there. Though I couldn't know it at the time, the spiritual feelings I experienced while diving were preparing me to move away from the Baptist church as the defining spiritual element of my life.

In Lexington, I immersed myself in the world of design and renovation, overseeing the conversion of the mill and lumberyard into a miniature mall of ten upscale shops, their fronts done in the Colonial style of Williamsburg, Virginia.

So I was now an antique dealer, which meant I simply *had* to make a yearly trip to London with my store manager to buy antiques and ship them home by the container load. That annual expedition fed my love of travel, my love for antiques, and my passion for negotiating—"horse trading," as Daddy called it. One of my favorite books of that era was Donald Trump's *The Art of Negotiation*, which for me was like reading a thriller.

The work of transforming the mill and lumberyard was an outlet for my long unused creative genius. I felt tremendously engaged in the design process, and I thrilled to see my architectural visions becoming reality. Having grown up with a father who built whatever he envisioned, I wasn't intimidated by what turned out to be an enormous undertaking. I built an office for myself above the antique shop where I watched with pride as my venture succeeded.

I sold more than half of our land, which had become ultra-desirable residential property, and Esther and I put our energies into renovating and redecorating the manor, with its elaborate amenities. She and I worked especially well together when it came to interior design and decoration, sharing as we did a taste for simple elegance and English antiques. Transforming that house together was one of the great joys of our long partnership.

When I was fifty-eight, Esther and I entered therapy again, and would continue together in some form of counseling for the next four years. We shared the belief that our faith in God, combined with the intercession of professional therapists, could solve any emotional problems confronting us as well as problems we were unaware of. This time, though, I was determined to use therapy for more than getting through a difficult phase of our marriage. I wanted to understand myself more deeply and find out, if possible, what made me tick.

This time I discussed some of my sexual history. With the therapist's encouragement I revealed to Esther and our children that I had been troubled by homosexual feelings during my adolescence and young adulthood. I also told them that I had made a conscious decision in college to willfully overcome my attraction to men and to live a traditional heterosexual life.

To my surprise and bewilderment, my family did not seem to hear me as I divulged my long-held secrets. How strange! It was as if the nature of my revelation were so far removed from their expectations of me as to be inconceivable, and therefore inaudible. I was very disappointed that no one said a word in response to my confession. Looking back on that moment of extreme vulnerability, I understand that I was longing for catharsis or for words of support from my family. When it became clear, however, that the truth of my past was unacceptable to them, I stuffed it back inside and spoke of it no more.

Throughout all my years of marriage, I remained a dedicated and enthusiastic member of our church. I was a member and chairman of all the major church committees, my favorite being the music committee. Under my leadership we raised the money for the installation of a new pipe organ that brought great notoriety to the church, with E. Power Biggs playing the inaugural concert.

Our home was frequently the site of important church functions and social events. We often entertained upwards of 150 people, my purview being the decorating of the house, caring for the garden, and creating flower arrangements of home-grown blooms. Esther undertook the formidable task of overseeing the preparation and serving of mountains of food. We were unquestionably the grand entertainers of the church; both born to our roles; both reveling in sharing our good fortune with our community.

But something was wrong, something as yet unclear, yet undeniable. In our late fifties, the chasm between Esther and me reopened and widened; I often felt that she wanted everything about our life to remain fixed, while I desperately wanted it to open up and become something new. Esther saw us gradually shifting our focus to being grandparents and church elders, with me continuing in business as her father had. Sadly, I felt myself mired in sameness, my spirit suffocating. In the absence of our children, the last child grown and gone from the nest, Esther and I could no longer deny the seriousness of our conflict.

I was grateful for all I had accomplished and for all that God had given me, yet I felt deeply dissatisfied. I longed for transformation, and my prayers reflected this longing. There is an old saying, "Be careful what you pray for because you just might get it." And so it was that my prayers for change and transformation were to be answered in ways I could never have imagined.

28
My Crucifixion

In 1989, as I approached my sixtieth birthday, a new associate pastor joined our congregation. Edwin was thirty-three, movie-star handsome, a powerful, charismatic preacher, and a natural showman. I was immediately drawn to him, though I had no conscious thought of sexual attraction. Impressed by his passionate, straightforward preaching, I invited him to have lunch with me. Our connection was immediate and electric, as if we had known each other for many years, the bond between us already well established. Soon thereafter, I realized that I'd found more than a friend, I had found a *best* friend and soul mate. That Edwin felt the same way about me was exactly the emotional boost I needed.

Without our children at home, Esther was essentially "unemployed," our entire modus operandi dramatically altered. Our children had formed the great bond between us, but who were we, separately and together, without children? What was our purpose in life? I began to keep a journal of my thoughts and feelings and prayers, much of my writing ignited by therapy. An excerpt from 1990: *So many unresolved issues between us. I want healthy, independent bonding. Our therapist calls it "interdependence."*

Meanwhile, with Esther urging me on, I liquidated and closed the antique shop. My journal chronicles my emphatic efforts to simplify life and lift some of the heavier responsibilities from my shoulders.

The sale was a great success, exceeding all my expectations. I feel distance growing between Esther and me as I continue with such openness and vigor in counseling and she has a different pace. I'm really afraid, yet I feel so alive — like life beginning. O God, I pray we will not grow further apart. I want balance for my life; "balance" is the word for 1990. God and spiritual growth, work, play, education, travel, friends. Balance with growth — the theme for '90. Thank you, God, for this insight. I know you have a mission for me and I am ready for the journey.

The sale is over, the building closed. Now to Cayman alone for a few days. Perfect timing. Need space from everything and everyone. Seven-mile-long beach walks — need even more. I'm writing this under my security blanket — the pine on the beach. Awakened at 6 A.M. with many concerns — control, abandonment, aging. Assumed an attitude of prayer — feel more relaxed now. Remember: openness, willingness, sensitivity, and balance.

God, I trust you and the process, which is painfully slow. I do need direction.

It was at this critical juncture that Edwin entered my life. I was thrilled to have a friend so intelligent and charming and fun. He and his wife and Esther and I occasionally did things together as couples, but Edwin and I saw each other several times a week as workout partners, lunch buddies, and confidants. That the interdependence I longed to create with Esther came effortlessly and naturally in my relationship with Edwin highlighted the growing tension between Esther and me.

Edwin also had a profound impact on our congregation. He was instantaneously popular with the younger members, especially the women, and just as immediately *unpopular* with many of the older, more conservative members, many of whom frowned upon our friendship. They considered our apparent intimacy and enjoyment of each other inappropriate, and threatening to the rigid social proprieties of our congregation.

Friendship—brotherly love—was holy according to Christ, and my friendship with Edwin was precisely brotherly. Indeed, the fact that he and I could be so close without any sexual overtones was liberating for me. Today, in this supposedly more enlightened era, a friendship between an older man and a much younger man still raises eyebrows. Even among open-minded progressives, there is an assumption that in a bond between men of greatly disparate ages, something other than friendship must be at the heart of the matter—money, sex, power. What many people don't seem to realize is that true friendship is founded on the recognition in each other of ageless wonders, ageless joys, and ageless similarities. Edwin inspired me to stop thinking of myself as a man tottering on the brink of old age. He gave me, literally, a new lease on life.

The story of the pony-cart accident illustrates Edwin's formidable influence over me. On my sixty-first birthday, barely a year after he and I became friends, I was in a near-catastrophic accident with my six-year-old grandson. I had begun raising Welsh ponies. We had eight of the spirited little horses trained to pull two-wheeled carts—lightweight chariots—and I loved driving them around the estate. As I was gaily rolling along in one of these with my grandson, the left wheel froze; this panicked the pony, which bolted, causing the cart to flip over. My grandson and I went to the hospital in the same ambulance, he with a deep cut on his head, I with three cracked ribs.

The next morning, as I lay convalescing with the help of painkillers, Edwin called, not to console me, but to say, "Well, are you gonna let this little setback make an old man of you?" Piqued by his challenge, I went to the gym the very next day, grateful to Edwin for getting me off my butt. I recognized in him that youthful, daring part of me that I'd suppressed for much of my life.

Meanwhile, I was beginning to feel the cumulative exhaustion of more than thirty years' toil in service to the church. I was asked to be the chairman of the deacons for a second time—an unprecedented honor and responsibility—which meant that I would be chairing the pulpit committee in our search for a new pastor. Talking things over with Esther, I confessed, "I'm tired, burned out. I don't want to take on all this new stuff. I need a break, not more responsibility."

To which she adamantly replied, "But you *have* to do it. Who else has the organizational skills and the ability to work with all the different factions?"

My early rise to leadership positions in the church was due directly to the prominence of Esther's father in the congregation. Upon his death I took his place as a trustee of a prestigious Baptist seminary, a position I would hold for seventeen years. I labored there with the certainty that the seminary had an impact beyond the local church, with our graduates carrying our message around the world.

I could not hope to match my father-in-law's financial contributions to the seminary, but Esther and I gave as generously as we could.

I had been groomed to carry on my father's work in the world. I had escaped that fate by allying myself with my wife's father. However, my escape proved to be more of a transfer. For twenty years I was the keeper, as it were, of my father-in-law's flame. It was no easy matter to move away from these inherited positions, and decades of daily involvement with the church drained me.

Our congregation was, in its adherence to the old ways, deeply patriarchal. Esther was neither inclined to assume her father's role in the church, nor would she have been allowed to. The feminist movement barely penetrated our church, though I pushed hard to get the nominating committee to nominate women as deacons. It was a great day in Baptist history when we elected the first woman deacon, and I'm proud to have done my part in bringing about that breakthrough.

So I went against my better judgment and took on more work for the church, ignoring the growing animosity toward me as a result of my continuing and deepening relationship with Edwin. It seemed to me that gaining a dear friend through my church was an affirmation of God's love. Where else should I have found my best friend? Homophobia, I would soon learn, was more virulent than ever among fundamentalist Christians in the 1990s. I was, however, so wrapped up in work, church, marriage, and friendship that gay politics was as removed from my life as the distant planets.

Indeed, so confident was I in my identity as a straight man that, for the first thirty years of my association with the church, I happily participated in the woman-less talent shows that were important fundraisers for our church. If you've never heard of these talent shows, you're probably not from the South, where woman-less weddings and talent shows were fundraising mainstays of many organizations. I had participated in such weddings in high school, singing "I Love You Truly" and "Because" in my gorgeous falsetto while wearing an evening gown fitted to me by its owner, Miss Mary. The central "joke" driving these events is that all the participants are male, most of them performing in drag.

In my last talent show, circa 1991, before a crowd of several hundred Baptists, I had my back to the audience as the curtain parted. I turned slowly to face them and the congregation exploded with laughter at the sight of me dressed as a nun, and not just any nun, but a pregnant one. At the height of the communal hysteria, I ran down off the stage and sat in the pastor's lap. I experienced a vague uneasiness about playing the part of a woman in front of hundreds of homophobic Baptists, and I decided not to participate in these burlesques again.

But my discretion did not extend to my friendship with Edwin. For the first time in my life, I was enjoying a relationship founded on unconditional love. Edwin's words to me were, "There is nothing you can say or do or be that would alter my love for you." This has remained my definition of unconditional love; I have expressed it to my children, and I love them exactly as they are.

Still, there was no denying that Edwin's extreme self-confidence coupled with his popularity among the younger members made him an enemy of the old guard. And, of course, there were those who had been jealous of me and my relative wealth and success for decades. I ignored them as I had ignored such people all my life, little suspecting that my growing closeness to Edwin was just what they had been waiting for to bring me down. We were aware that there was gossip about us in the halls, but we didn't take it seriously.

I don't know who started the rumors, though I have my suspicions, but in the chaotic days of the search for a new pastor, church gossip began to include allusions to something more than mere friendship between Jody and Edwin — something wicked and unforgivable. Why else, the bitter tongues wagged, would such a prominent member of the Baptist community, a major contributor to the church's financial well-being, and head of the committee entrusted with finding a new pastor, spend so much time with a man in his thirties?

As these rumors swirled through our congregation, Esther and I went to the Cayman Islands to celebrate thirty-eight years of marriage. We didn't have much of a celebration; communication between us was at low ebb. One evening after supper, Esther asked me quite abruptly, "Do you want a divorce?" I said no, but the tension and discomfort between us remained. Counseling had failed to solve our dilemma of how to happily coexist and expand our world together in the absence of our children.

Upon our return to Lexington, finding the rumors of my involvement with Edwin more virulent than ever, I asked Esther, "Do you think I'm gay?"

"No, I do not," she replied calmly, and we spoke no more of it. Knowing that she had answered me honestly made me rest easier, for what Esther felt about me was a hundred times more important than any judgment of me from outside our union.

Then, three years after Edwin entered my life, there came a monthly business meeting in the church dining hall, attended by some 400 members of the congregation. With no pastor in place, I, as chairman of the deacons, was to be chairman. I went to the microphone to call the meeting to order. Suddenly, a group of about twenty people sitting at tables in the center section of the hall began to hiss and boo. I was stunned into silence as the hissing and booing grew louder, and a venomous cloud of hatred crawled along the floor and up onto the stage where it engulfed me.

I waited for someone, anyone, to rise to my defense, but no one did. I hoped that the great majority of the people would protest; that someone would stand up and shout, "Stop that!" or at least "What is the meaning of this?" But no one made the slightest move to intervene. After suffering that hateful onslaught for what seemed an eternity, I returned to my seat and waited for the hissing to subside. Then, to my astonishment, a well-respected retired pastor asked me to continue moderating the meeting. I looked at him and said, "The chairman of the deacons refuses to moderate." Then I left the hall in a state of shock and anger—hurt to my core.

Esther had come to the meeting in a separate car; moments after I got home, she drove up. I expected her to be sympathetic and supportive, but instead she was angry with me. Before I could say a word, she asked, "Why did you refuse to be the moderator?"

"You're not aware of what went on before that?" I replied, shocked by her coldness.

"Yes, but that's no excuse," she said, frowning. "I was embarrassed and ashamed."

I gazed at her in disbelief. To be crucified by the primitive faction of my church was bad enough, but to be forsaken by my wife was a stab in the heart. At that moment, we separated. We would never share a bed again. I realized that Esther was wed to the church, not to me. Seeing where her deeper loyalty lay, I felt the last bonds between us sundered.

A few weeks later, after another in a long line of sleepless nights, I chaired the meeting of the pulpit committee, concluding the proceedings by reading my letter of resignation from that committee and from the church. I reminded those forty people of my thirty-six years of devotion to the congregation, and of the loving hours I gave each week to keep our church a dynamic and solvent witness in our region. I shared my sorrow at being so unjustly maligned and humiliated by false rumors and accusations. When I finished reading, there was complete silence. Shocked anew by the lack of support, I left the room, about to explode.

An older member and friend caught up to me at the elevator. He pleaded with me to change my mind. "No," I said. "It's too late. When I was booed you did nothing to stop them from attacking me. Where were you when I needed you?"

Then I drove to a quiet place by the river and fell apart, utterly devastated, sobbing uncontrollably, yet, when my tears finally abated, I felt a surprising sense of relief.

In the wake of my resignation, the chairman of the personnel committee asked Edwin to resign his position as associate pastor. Edwin called to tell me they had offered him the absolute minimum severance pay. Hearing this, I called the chairman of personnel and the chairman of finance and asked them to come to my office. When they arrived, I looked at each of them and said, "You will give Edwin a decent severance package or I will sue the church—and you know I will." Wanting to avoid a scandal, they greatly improved Edwin's settlement. As I expected, my threat to sue was taken by my enemies as proof of my sinful alliance with Edwin.

I had never wanted to take on the responsibilities of again becoming chairman of the deacons, knowing that our by-laws would also require me to become chairman of the impending pastor search. Had I trusted my intuition and been self-confident enough to overcome Esther's entreaties, all of this might have been avoided. Perhaps some other pretext for attacking me would have been found; some other excuse for trying to crush what they mistook for sin.

It is little wonder that I no longer belong to any formal

religious community. I now focus my meditations on my personal feelings for God and Nature. I believe God's love for all of us is unconditional. Any religious order that portrays God's love as restricted or limited misses the boat—the infinitely huge boat of God's love.

29
Now It's My Turn

Dissolving my relationship with my church — my primary society of thirty-six years — filled me with anger and sorrow that would stay with me for many years. Fortunately, my faith was unshaken. I no longer needed a fixed place of worship, nor any dogma to commune with God. Having been blessed throughout life with direct experiences of the mystical nature of reality, I believed in a supreme intelligence and power — God — transcending human-made concepts.

Ending my marriage was another matter. For all our differences, Esther and I had been best friends, our bond forged in the fires of parenthood and a shared devotion to God and community. We had carried each other through the greatest grief parents can endure, and had shared all the joys and challenges of raising children together. We had given our best to each other for nearly four decades, forging a prosperous life for our children and ourselves. Together. Always together. And now we were splitting apart.

Within a few days of what I refer to as my crucifixion at the hands of my congregation, I gave a month's notice to the couple renting the little apartment in our barn. Esther and I then suffered along together in the main house for four long weeks, her domain upstairs, mine downstairs. The tension between us unbearable, we made every effort not to intersect. I felt terrible at the huge distance now between us, yet it was obvious that I'd long needed my own space and ample quiet in which to ponder what to do next.

When I was finally able to move into the simple three-room barn apartment, I collapsed into sleep. For the first several days I slept twelve hours a night and took long midday naps. I soon realized that I was making up for more than a few months of sleep deprivation, but for *years* of unreleased tension. By the end of my first week in the barn I was certain there would be no reconciliation with Esther. Despite the emotional chaos swirling around me, I felt very much at peace living alone.

And so, at the age of sixty-two, I began to clear the boards for the creation of the life *I* wanted. It was as if I had returned to that emotional moment forty-three years earlier when I landed my Piper Cub and strode to the pay phone to tell my father of my triumphant flight back to Athens. Only this time, instead of commanding me to stop flying, he said, "Congratulations. Now you are free."

Indeed, shortly after I moved into the barn, I called Daddy and told him about my split with Esther. "I'm not surprised," he said calmly. "You and Esther are so different."

"But I never mentioned anything to you about a conflict between us," I said, surprised by his reaction.

"Yes, but I knew," he said quietly.

I see now how appropriate it was that he was aware of my schism with Esther, for he had maintained the outer semblance of harmony with my mother for decades, when in reality they had lived together at a far greater emotional remove than Esther and I ever had.

The barn apartment was a perfect setting for beginning my new life. The large kitchen and living room were downstairs, bedroom and bathroom upstairs. Above my bedroom was the barn attic, home to a family of opossums, their latest litter born shortly after I moved in. There were many nights when I settled down to sleep just as my upstairs neighbors—with scritching and scratching and opossum whispering—embarked on their nocturnal activities.

I joked that I lived in the manger—no room at the inn—my only companions being horses and varmints, but I spoke only half in jest. Edwin had moved to Cincinnati and taken a "civilian" job, his Baptist credentials now tainted. In the absence of my church community, I found that I had few good friends and no one to whom I could confide my deeper feelings. Edwin had been brother, friend, and confidant. Though he and I frequently talked by phone, I was essentially on my own.

One Sunday afternoon, a few months after settling into the barn, I received a call from a Baptist minister from another congregation, a man I knew through intra-church gatherings, and professionally, too, as I had leased a car to him. I was a bit puzzled about his calling me at home, but my puzzlement quickly turned to shock when he said, "I heard that Edwin moved out of town. I thought you might be lonely for a good time. I'm sure we could give each other pleasure."

"You are mistaken," I said curtly. "I am straight. Please don't call again."

This call exposed what I had long known to be true; that the ministry of the Baptist church was rife with closeted gay men. More important, it affirmed my conscious desire to live my life as a heterosexual. I considered my attraction to men a malady in need of curing, and I hoped that new liaisons with women would prove to be that cure.

My two years in the barn gave me lots of alone time to gain a sense of myself unattached to anyone else. The importance of this cannot be overstated. Equally meaningful was the discovery that I no longer required the material trappings of success I'd become accustomed to. My minimalist furnishings and the extreme pleasure I felt in simple living helped me realize that no amount of possessions could provide me inner peace, which was what I craved more than anything else.

Once I moved into the barn, Esther and I had almost no direct contact. I spent my days at my office or running the farm, while Esther lived on in the main house. The daily pattern of her life barely changed after we separated. When we did meet, she would ask me, "Do you want a divorce?" At first I said no, then after some months I said maybe, and after a year I finally said yes.

When it was absolutely clear to both of us that our split was going to be permanent, I went shopping for a lawyer. All during the process, and for some months after the papers were filed, I used the phrase, "The legal documents are pending," instead of the "D" word.

The pragmatism that characterized the beginning of our marriage characterized our divorce as well. Though there was much to sort out, our dissolution was largely free of rancor; Esther trusted me to be fair about the division of our properties, and I wanted her to have everything she really wanted. Our divorce was final seven months after the process began; completing the final property dissolution took another five years.

I made it clear to our children from the outset that I still respected their mother, cared about her well-being, and wanted only the best for her. As we had been united in our devotion to our children, Esther and I chose not to make villains of each other. I will be forever grateful that our children were not asked to make any kind of a choice between us. My children were, and are to this day, the greatest blessings of my life.

While waiting for the divorce to become final, Edwin and I went on a five-week road trip across America. He too was recently divorced, and between jobs. We hopped into a brand-new, bright red Bonneville SSE and headed west. This was the first time in my life I traveled anywhere without making arrangements for lodging in advance. By the end of that first week, I was reveling in the fun and magic of spontaneity. Ever since then, I've been a much more relaxed and flexible traveler.

In San Francisco, passing a Delta Airlines ticket office, I turned to Edwin and asked, "Ever been to Alaska?"

"No," he said. "I've always wanted to go."

"I've never been either," I said, guiding him into the ticket office. "Let's go now."

We were like kids on a spree. We drove fast, drank too much, changed our minds at the drop of a hat, and laughed more than I've ever laughed. Despite eight speeding tickets, we made it back safely to Kentucky, our friendship stronger than ever.

On the afternoon my divorce decree became final, I entered a tattoo parlor frequented by sailors and prostitutes and had a fantastic eagle emblazoned on my skin in a place where only my most intimate friends would ever see it. The eagle has always represented freedom for me. Having that powerful symbol tattooed on me on that particular day, despite the pain involved, seemed the perfect way to commemorate freedom from my old way of life.

A few weeks later, I had a powerful impulse to fly to England. Struck by the realization that I was truly beholden only to myself, I booked a flight for later that same day. As I was packing, I looked in the mirror and saw a man wearing a wig. I glared at my reflection and said, "This is not who I am." I flung my hairpiece into the wastebasket. Publicly bald for the first time in twenty years, I realized that my hairpiece had been a major part of my disguise—the lid of my false identity. How nice it was to walk the streets of London free of the weight of that obligatory rug, scalp tingling at the caress of the cooling air.

My two years in the barn came to an end when Esther purchased her own home and moved out of the main house. I then moved into the main house, furnished a few rooms, and left the rest empty. I resided there for another year until I sold the house along with fifty acres. I then bought a large new house adjoining my remaining 150 acres. Settled in a new home, I began splitting my time between Kentucky and my apartment in the Caymans—the one property I'd been most eager to retain.

As I started to feel solidly single again, I met several women, some of whom I dated, some of whom I both dated and traveled with. Because I had no interest in fathering more children, and heeding Daddy's renewed warnings not to impregnate some sweet young gold digger, I had a vasectomy. When I told Daddy I'd been snipped, he smiled broadly and breathed a sigh of relief.

I felt no great urge to wed again; in many ways I preferred being single. I had come to cherish being alone. I've made a point of giving myself time alone every day, sometimes for several days at a time. One of my personal commandments has become *Do Not Fear Aloneness,* for in quiet communion with ourselves we can connect more deeply with our own inner wisdom and the wisdom of God.

30
Diving and Dancing

My wildest days of freedom awaited in the Caymans. In due course, I sold the mall and the remaining acreage of our farm, and then sold my auto dealership to my son. Shorn of all but a few Kentucky responsibilities, and having convinced Edwin to move with me, I made my principal residence the Cayman Islands. What would we do there? Scuba dive, dance, party, and build and operate a fast-food Mexican restaurant.

Was I attracted to Edwin? Yes. Was there ever a hint of sexual interaction between us? No. Edwin, as it happened, was extremely homophobic. We were both exclusively involved with women, he far more than I.

I connected mostly with women I knew from the mainland who came to the island for a visit, or whose company I sought when island fever propelled me back to the mainland. Edwin and I did some adventuring together before the restaurant opened, our greatest excursion a trip to Europe. Spontaneity continued to be our hallmark.

My favorite island activities were diving and dancing. We dove several times a week until the restaurant was up and running, every dive a dance with God. Edwin often dove at night, but it was not my bliss. I dove to be embraced by the *visible* miracle of the water, to be dazzled by the light, to see the incredible vistas of the underwater world, to feel embraced by Nature. I saved the night for dancing.

Every evening until the restaurant opened, and thereafter twice a week, I would walk barefoot along the beach to the Holiday Inn beach bar and dance the night away to island music played by their wonderful house band. After forty years of restraining myself, there I was, barefoot and fancy-free, dancing on the beach in a tropical paradise. What a scene! Tourists and locals sipped margaritas in the warm Caribbean night, dancing and flirting and sharing the magic. The two songs I loved more than any others were *Tequila* and *Hot, Hot, Hot*. I generally danced to those tunes without a partner because I wanted the freedom to go absolutely wild, and I always did.

I always danced with Lois when the band played *Big Belly Man*. When that song would begin, Lois and I would turn to look for each other, our eyes would meet, and we'd converge on the dance floor. Isn't that a big part of what makes a community—finding those special ways to relate to each other that glue us all together and make everyone feel loved?

Edwin bedded women at a prodigious rate; he was a self-proclaimed sexual athlete, his choice of mates wide ranging.

Our largest challenge as housemates was Edwin's sexual

activity. When he was ensconced with a lover, I found it virtually impossible to be there. We began to arrange our trysts so that I would be on the mainland when he was entertaining, and vice-versa.

After nearly a year on the island, we opened our restaurant. That first Christmas, I invited all my children to come down for the holidays to see their old man's new business; I wanted to prepare and serve them our tacos with my own hands. While they were visiting, it occurred to me that while *my* Kentucky residence was a brand-new five-bedroom house, my oldest son was living with his wife and three children in a much smaller and older house. Feeling certain that I'd be living on the island for some time to come, I proposed we swap our Kentucky homes. My son and his wife slept on the proposal and said yes the following morning.

That small hundred-year-old house on sixteen acres remains my old Kentucky home to this day, my last toehold in the South, and the last chunk of arable land I own. It's in my blood to own land; I've had a lifelong romance with land and all the things that grow from it and live upon it.

Old habits die hard. Once the restaurant became a reality, I resumed my workaholic habits, spending long hours every day on the job. Edwin worked with me at the restaurant for the first few months, but then made the transition to working at home on his computer. keeping the books and handling payroll. I undertook hard physical labor, on my feet twelve to fourteen hours a day, striving, as always, for perfection.

The restaurant was a great success. When the health department would come to inspect the premises, the inspector would always say, "I can find nothing to cite you for. You have the cleanest restaurant on the island. But we have to find *something*." He would then make up some tiny infraction so his superiors wouldn't accuse him of shirking his duty.

Why, at age sixty-five, was I driving myself so hard? Because I wanted to prove to *myself* that I could succeed at a wholly new venture, having had no prior experience in the restaurant business, and in a foreign country to boot! I also found the process exciting and challenging. I loved starting from scratch and creating success. Breaking away from my old life had filled me with tremendous energy, most of which I poured into the restaurant. I celebrated my sixty-fifth birthday with Edwin and several of our diving friends—and yes, I danced the Charleston at the stroke of midnight.

In my position as a foreigner operating a business, I felt compelled to live more cautiously than many of my contemporaries. The following tale is a case is point.

Heidi, a very desirable German woman, came every night to the Holiday Inn accompanied by her native Caymanian boyfriend, a well-connected businessman. Heidi's German husband was a prominent island businessman, too, but he didn't go out with Heidi at night. Heidi was a marvelous dancer, and she and I were frequent salsa partners. She sunbathed every day, too, and I often stopped to chat with her. She flirted shamelessly with me. I enjoyed her attentions, but didn't take her flirting seriously.

Then one night, after a particularly rousing stint of salsa dancing, she asked me to *please* take her to my place. I drove her to my apartment. After a quick tour of the place, we entered the bedroom where serious kissing ensued. "Make love to me *now*!" she said, dragging me to the bed. But just as I was about to abandon myself to mindless passion, a voice inside my head shouted, *Be careful, Jody. She's got a jealous island boyfriend and a very unhappy husband.*

I stopped mid-kiss and said, "This feels too risky for me. Why don't we meet at your place in Miami away from all this island intrigue."

Diving and Dancing

Heidi was, to say the least, miffed at my refusal to go any further. When I drove her home and dropped her off, I spied her Caymanian boyfriend waiting for her in his car. I broke out in a cold sweat as I drove home, mightily relieved that I hadn't succumbed to her considerable charms. She was never friendly to me thereafter.

After two years' toil at the restaurant, I was physically burned out; island life had become much more work than play. When an appropriate opportunity to sell came along, I jumped at it. The sale coincided with Edwin and me both coming down with debilitating cases of island fever; even paradise can get a bit claustrophobic. A promising business venture arose in Orlando, Florida, and we moved there to take our chances together one more time.

By this time, Edwin had narrowed his amorous activities considerably, focusing his attentions on an extremely wealthy woman who was just crazy about Edwin and had a straightforward desire to woo him away from me. To that end she bought a mansion in Atlanta shortly before we made the move to Orlando. It was clear from the outset that the offer she was going to make him was going to beat mine hands down.

I bought our hotel-advertising business for one reason: to provide Edwin and me a way to make a good living. The plan was we would work together for a year or so to get the business established, and then I would bow out of the daily operations. The potential income—had Edwin been willing to work his butt off—was enormous. But his lover offered him a life of wealth and ease in exchange for his companionship—no hard work required. Eight months into our Orlando adventure, eight months into the ninth year of our relationship, Edwin left me alone in Orlando and went off to start a new life in Atlanta.

My children have never understood my connection to Edwin. They see him as a gigolo who took advantage of my love and generosity. But that's not what he was to me. I believe Edwin and I were brought together to help each other rescue those hidden, friendless boys who'd been hiding inside us most of our lives. We were liberators for each other. I will always feel that Edwin, through his unconditional love, helped me take several of my biggest strides along the path to emotional healing.

Less than a year after Edwin and I parted, I made the decision to embark on a course of deep therapy. I was fed up with falsity, and sad and angry that I'd never experienced a completely honest and sexually intimate relationship. I believed that if I could "cure myself" of the deeper maladies afflicting my psyche, I might yet have a deeply intimate relationship with a woman.

In our last year on the island, I read a book about a therapeutic technique of emotional release that many people were finding incredibly healing and transformative. Intrigued by the method as it was described in the book, I made a vow that one day I would undergo that form of therapy. And so, when Edwin left me, nothing and no one remained to keep me from making the move west to begin the work of healing myself.

31
Release and Rebirth

I like to compare therapy to peeling an onion. Every time you remove one layer, you find another beneath it. You peel that next layer away and there's another. And you're crying all the time. Eventually, if you have enough courage and stamina, you get down to the core of your emotions, to the founding experiences and patterns of your life.

The form of therapy I signed up for at age sixty-nine was all about the expression of feelings, combined with the active *physical* expulsion of grief and rage; there was almost no emphasis on the cognitive process; there was very little analysis or intellectualizing. Concepts of right and wrong, good and bad were disallowed. While I often had tremendous anxiety about going to therapy, I never canceled an appointment or was a no-show. Trusting the unknown, however frightened I felt, was a major part of my commitment to healing.

I saw my therapist every day for the first three weeks, and thereafter three times a week, each of our sessions lasting between two and three hours. My therapist's primary function was to encourage me to stay with my feelings as I talked, and to guide me without interpretation through deep emotional waters. When feelings of sorrow and rage would erupt—and they inevitably did—the therapist would act as my coach, urging me to keep going, to get my feelings out, to scream and rage and pound the walls and floors, and to verbalize my feelings as I released them.

At the end of each session I would try to sum up what I'd been through. I very much wanted my therapist to give me his take on what had just happened, but he would point out that I had all the answers I needed within me; his job was to facilitate my clearing away the emotional logjams blocking the healthy flow of my feelings.

I wrote in my journal after each session, fully immersed in the process of self-discovery—even in my sleep. Writing was another way of moving my feelings *out* of me. Being able to read the words and hear my story at a distance helped defuse some of the frightening power in the traumas of my past.

The same sort of emotional release I experienced in individual sessions was supposed to go on during the two weekly group sessions I attended, but I seldom felt I accomplished much meaningful work there. For me, the work of emotional release was difficult enough without the distractions of group work. I was often impatient and bored. There is a particular kind of neurotic, commonly known as a therapy junkie, who gravitates to and inhabits therapeutic situations with seemingly no hope or committed intention of improving or of completing the process. After all, one of my largest lifelong issues was that I had felt compelled to diminish my needs for the needs of others. Group therapy often felt like a continuation of that self-denial.

Then again, I was in the unusual and enviable position of being able to make therapy my full-time work, which is how I thought of it. I wasn't addicted to therapy, didn't use it as a crutch for limping through life, and never intended to remain in therapy year after year without end. I had the single-minded determination to forge ahead every day until the source of my misery was exposed and defused once and for all.

I was *never* bored during individual sessions. My initial focus, to return to the onion metaphor, was working my way through the layer of pain and rage I felt as a result of my crucifixion at the hands of my church brethren. I pounded the padded walls and screamed until I'd lost my voice, soaking my clothes with tears and sweat several times a week until I'd cleansed myself of the last residue of that trauma. And all through that release I felt absolutely certain that my suffering had nothing to do with God, but only with human ignorance and avarice.

Then I got to Esther and all the feelings I had stuffed in relation to her for so many years. I often felt enormous rage about her, but didn't mourn the end of our relationship nearly as much as I grieved the loss of our family, our magic circle of love. Indeed, therapy provided the revelation that, on a deep emotional level, Esther and I had remained strangers throughout our marriage.

I don't want to suggest that the course of my therapy unfolded in a neat and orderly fashion. Sometimes I would enter the room, flop down on the floor and say, "I don't have a clue. Help me." To which my therapist would reply, "Just get situated. It'll come out." Once the floodgates were opened, memories of past traumas rushed to the surface in no particular order.

As a stranger in the strange land of Los Angeles, I was fortunate to make the acquaintance of a remarkable man named Merlin shortly after moving there. We met as the result of my search for a massage therapist. Having a weekly massage is one of the reasons I've been able to stay relatively sane during the more stressful times. I've adhered to that practice for more than thirty years. Finding myself far from my Kentucky masseur, I answered an ad for deep massage that featured the phrase "oasis overlooking beach."

Merlin not only provided an oasis, but he also turned out to be from Kentucky. He was, among other things, a professional singer and had sung in my church! We were both excited and happy to have found a fellow southerner we could spend time with, and so it became our habit to have dinner together after my massage. Merlin was my first openly gay friend. Though there was nothing at all sexual about our friendship, I am sure that getting to know Merlin was enormously important in expanding my notion of life's possibilities.

Five months into my intense regimen of therapy, as I was about to begin an individual session focusing on Edwin and my feelings of being abandoned by him, I experienced a sharp tightness in my chest. This was not unusual before a session, nor was my elevated pulse of 125, but by the end of a session the tightness was usually gone, my pulse normal. Not so on that day. *After* the session my pulse was up to 135, the tightness in my chest persisting.

The therapist urged me to see a doctor immediately. I drove to Santa Monica where the doctor gave me some pills to relax me. I went home and took my blood pressure and heart rate. They were about normal, but the tightness in my chest would not go away. After a long, restless night, I went to the emergency room and was examined by a cardiologist. His diagnosis was that I had suffered a heart attack. I immediately checked into a hospital. Once my condition was stabilized, I decided to have bypass surgery in Lexington, where my children would be nearby to visit me and help with my recuperation.

Two and a half months after successful surgery and a wonderful bonding experience with my children, I returned to Los Angeles and resumed therapy. My focus returned to Edwin's abandoning me. At the height of my fury, I remembered a workshop I had attended in Lexington the year before I met Edwin. Dr. Bernie Siegel had us draw pictures of our lives and ourselves as we saw them in that moment. He said, "Put your heart and your brain in the picture somewhere." He exhorted us to be totally honest. No one else had to see the picture.

I drew myself in the grasp of a horrible black octopus with one red eye at its heart, its tentacles covering my body. I was shocked by how grotesque the picture was, and I knew it was a depiction of my sexual confusion. I was choked with emotion and had difficulty breathing. On the verge of tears, I struggled to keep from sobbing in that big room surrounded by 200 strangers. A decade later in Los Angeles, my heart repaired, I was ready to do battle with that octopus, still believing that if I could annihilate it, I would finally be free.

Those were extremely difficult months of therapy, in which memories of my mother and father became the focal point of my experience. Urged on by my therapist, I released oceans of rage and tears concerning my mother. I relived again and again that scene of Daddy riding away on his big horse, leaving little Jody on the porch, begging to be taken along, and that pain had to be exorcised, too.

But for all the old anger and suppressed feelings I released, I still felt helpless in the grip of my "sickness" that manifested as a desire to be sexually intimate with a man. I expressed repeatedly to my therapist that I couldn't go on like this, that it would be better to die than be tormented by what seemed to be an irresolvable flaw. In my journal of that time, I wrote, on more than one occasion, "perhaps there is no way out for me but death."

Then, about a year into therapy, at a Friday-night dance, a woman asked me to dance with her and then asked me out on a date. I was stricken with anxiety; raw and vulnerable from therapy, I didn't feel safe with women; I didn't trust them. I was immersed in memories of Mother and Esther and the various ways—subtle and overt—that they dominated me. Furthermore, I had become convinced that until I could resolve the question of my sexuality, *any* relationship with a woman was doomed. I wrote in my journal, "I must have hope to change."

Despite my trepidation, I went out to dinner with her. After a pleasant meal, she showed me a coupon book she'd purchased full of discounts at many fine restaurants in the area. Blithely, as if there could be no question of my response, she said, "Now that we've found each other, we can go to *all* these restaurants together." Aghast at her presumption, I never contacted her again.

Therapy made me more aware of my tendency to attract and gravitate to extremely strong and controlling women. My therapist, hearing of my desire to get over my fear of women and to find a suitable mate, encouraged me to date all kinds of women rather than limit myself to the more aggressive ones. In this way, he suggested, I could discover what type of woman I truly enjoyed being with.

That Halloween, I went to a therapy costume party dressed as a stick of dynamite: black sweatshirt and black pants, a fuse coming out of my red cap—covered with dozens of white *F*'s, for Failure. Literally wallowing in the shame dredged up in therapy, I was in the throes of believing I had failed as a father, feelings that engulfed me for weeks until I was able to work through them.

After a year with a male therapist, I switched to a female, whom I chose because she was nurturing, compassionate, and extremely sensitive—and because she was petite, feminine, charming, and French. Though not sexually attracted to her, I felt she was the *type* of woman I wanted to be with. The therapeutic technique remained the same, but the energy with her was different: I felt freer to express myself about my sexuality and my sexual history.

Three times in the course of therapy—once with the male therapist, twice with the female—I relived my excruciating passage from the womb into the birth canal. Starting in a place of deeply satisfying security, I entered a hot, claustrophobic passage where I was barely able to breathe. Curled in the fetal position, I kicked and pushed my way out of that crushing confinement into the first terrifying moments of life outside my mother.

The benefit of this process was that afterward I could remember many more events from early childhood. These rebirth experiences were so exhausting and emotionally draining, however, that after the third time I told the therapist, "No more of that." I have been told that if a therapist allows a patient to remain in the birth canal too long, the patient may suffer brain damage. Judging from the intensity and traumatic nature of my experiences, I don't doubt this.

Over the course of therapy, something began to gradually shift in me. The change was so subtle I was barely aware of it at first. I found it easier to talk about my sexual yearnings as a young man, and my feelings of shame about those yearnings decreased. I was also able to more fully express my sorrow and frustration about having spent a lifetime sacrificing my needs to please others.

My feelings of helplessness began to be supplanted by relief and gratitude. "I feel so fortunate to be here," I would say. "Thank God I had the wisdom to do this for *me*." Slowly but surely, the rage and despair about my conflicted sexuality changed to rage at religious and societal intolerance of who and what I wanted to be.

The exact moment of my sexual awakening would be impossible to pinpoint, but midway through the second year of therapy, I became aware that the confusion embodied in the question "What's wrong with me?" was fast being replaced by the sense that my desires were not unhealthy. On the contrary, *all* of my feelings and desires began to feel more and more natural, until one day I realized that I was virtually free of shame; there was *nothing* wrong with me. The misperceptions that had ruled me for seventy years had finally been replaced by the truth.

I believe that as I emptied myself of the tons of toxic anger I'd suppressed and stored inside for seventy years, the ensuing spaciousness allowed my sexuality to blossom and expand. In the absence of neurotic baggage, my sexuality was no longer compressed by shame. The context of unforgivable sin shifted to a deeply personal context of acceptance and love of self.

I was a man who loved men, a man who desired other men. For the first time in my life I felt safe enough to let myself *be* that without trying to deny it or run from it. Of course I was shy about my new identity at first, and still largely secretive outside the confines of therapy. But the unaltered acceptance of me by therapists and new friends reassured and encouraged me. "Why not be attracted to men, if that's who you're attracted to?" they all seemed to say. What's more, God did not strike me down. And every day that I openly acknowledged this truth, I felt better and better. How enslaved I had been by my misconceptions!

Having come out to myself, to Merlin, and to my therapist, those last six months of therapy were enormously important, if less dramatic than the preceding eighteen. Therapy provided me an intimate way to practice being my new self in the presence of my therapist. The absence of any great anger confirmed my feeling that those outbursts of rage at Esther in the early years of our marriage, and the regrettable outbursts at my children, had their source in my conflicted sexuality—my lifelong suppression of that sweet man who just wanted to be himself and love other men.

During one of my last sessions with my therapist, she made a brief speech that brought tears of joy to my eyes. Her simple words signified the end of my therapeutic journey—that leg of it anyway. "You don't seem to have any issues," she said with a smile. "Let's not make another appointment for now. Come again as you feel it's necessary."

So then the question became "What will I do with the truth?" I felt at peace in myself, but had yet to imagine how to proceed with my new awareness and newly discovered original identity.

The first loud answer to that question came during the last week of December 1999. To celebrate the coming of the year 2000, and in the tradition of my father, I took all my children and their families on a Caribbean cruise. On December 28, while everyone else went ashore at St. Lucia, I stayed in my cabin and spent several hours in deep meditation. I came to the conclusion—a divine revelation—that I had to tell the truth to my children and my sisters. Henceforth, I wanted to relate to them with complete honesty, and do away with all emotional obstacles between us.

I carried my determination to reveal the truth back to California and throughout the last months of full-time therapy. In June of 2000, I wrote a letter, which I sent to all my children, my sisters, and a close friend in Kentucky. I wrote the letter longhand; when I rewrote it, I changed only four words. I took that as a sign that I had it right, that the letter had come from a deep and true place. I then hand copied it for each of my children. Here is that letter.

As long as I can remember I have been attracted to men as well as to women. Every single day of my life I have struggled with the pain and confusion of "What's wrong with me?"

A significant part of who I am has been locked in a cage until now. I have given myself permission to unlock the cage and to be honest with you about who I really am.

As I begin to release the burden of this lifelong pain, and to be true to my feelings, I am scared about revealing my lifelong secret. However, I am prepared for whatever the consequences may be. I want so much to be at peace and harmony within myself for the years I have left.

Presently, I am not involved with anyone, nor do I have any plans about the future. I simply want to experience myself in serenity and freedom. God is with me and I do have faith to trust the unknown.

*THE PAST CANNOT BE CHANGED.
My love for you deepens and becomes more meaningful with time. You are so precious and dear to me.*
Dad

How did they respond? Each of my children and my sisters reacted differently and uniquely, some with ease and immediate acceptance, some with great difficulty, denial, and ambivalence. But now that the dust has settled, they have all come to accept and respect me as I am today. Though they may not completely understand me, they love me, and each has told me so without prompting.

Unconditional love is acceptance *without* having to understand everything about your beloved. I can say with absolute certainty that practicing unconditional love has created deeper bonds with my children and provided me the inner peace I've longed for since childhood. Loving unconditionally is certainly not always easy, but it nurtures the soul and warms the heart, and it is well worth the effort.

32
Jody Today

I live in Venice, California, a short walk from the ocean and a vast beach where I love to ramble. Though my home is a townhouse with only a small garden, I still "putter" in the soil enough to keep my green thumb exercised and to nurture my passion for the earth. Choosing to settle here was made easier by the preponderance of blooming camellias and azaleas—reminders of my southern Georgia roots and the happy hours I spent in my youth gardening with my mother.

    My townhouse is modestly appointed and contains a few of my favorite things from my old Kentucky home, but not many. I like keeping Kentucky in Kentucky. The frosting on the cake is the lagoon outside my window. Colorful koi patrol the waters, and many species of birds, both permanent and migratory, make this their home—a serene oasis amidst the busy millions around me. Nearly everyone who comes to visit me utters the word "paradise" within a few minutes of arriving.

I still return several times a year to my old Kentucky home on its sixteen acres—an ideal respite from urban life. There I commune with my family and a few dear friends. Occasionally, I travel farther south to connect with loved ones in Georgia. I am always filled with nostalgia when I return to the familiar haunts of my youth. Gratefully, with each visit my memories are more and more of the sweeter, joyful times, less and less of the sorrowful.

I love my life here in California. To wake each day without the emotional constriction of maintaining a false identity is an ongoing miracle. I love how my body feels in this temperate climate, and I thrive on the youthful energy that abounds here; the ambition of youth stimulates my desire to focus on the positive essence of everything I do, think, and feel. My spirits are buoyed by the colorful cosmopolitan mix of races that share this place, and I love the permissive nature of this society. To live among people who feel free to be themselves without fear of being condemned or attacked for their lifestyle choices is deeply reassuring.

And I have a dear friend in Angelo, who is my physical trainer, my fitness guru, my nutritionist, and my confidant. I continue to struggle with my weight, but Angelo is always patient as he guides me to eat more healthfully. Whatever happens in our respective lives, we are there for each other, sharing our unconditional love. Our companionship is an immeasurable solace.

No longer a practicing businessman, I still possess a formidable drive to be productive. I now attend regular acting classes in pursuit of a career in television commercials, and I have a wonderful connection with my commercial agent; I am his only grandfather client. I consider myself a late-blooming character actor, a vision of myself that both excites and inspires me.

I have also begun taking art classes to appease my creative artist self. Who knows? I may yet become a "Grandpa Moses."

Jody Today

My right brain finally has a chance to catch up with my left brain—the artist triumphant!

Having gone through bypass surgery, and suffering some of the inevitable infirmities that come with getting older, I breathe easier knowing that the best of cutting-edge medical resources are close at hand.

I am single at seventy-four. I continue to trust the unknown, to give myself permission to explore inward, and to revel in simple pleasures: spending time with family and friends, meditation, prayer, exercise, massage, travel, movie going, reading, horseback riding, scuba diving, and infrequent visits to my therapist.

Yes, I have my moments of despair and loneliness. I'm sometimes fearful of impending surgery, or worried about how I'll navigate the world if my vision continues to worsen. But with God's guidance, I remember to focus on what I *do* have—the joyful aspects of life—and I cease to worry.

I am reminded of Inga, a tall, pretty woman I met while living in the Cayman Islands. I can see her clearly in my mind's eye as she came to dance at the Holiday Inn every evening during the winter months. She owned a small cottage on the island; her principal residence was in Chicago. Inga always danced alone, her style modern freeform with a sprinkle of ballet. She danced barefoot, with marvelous grace. Whenever I watched her dance, I thought, *Poetry in motion.* She wore her long gray hair in a single braid, never wore a smidgen of makeup, and dressed in comfy ankle-length skirts with mismatched blouses. She was an original: confident, comfortable, self-contained, and very intriguing.

One night I felt moved to ask Inga to dance with me. She smiled faintly and reached out with both hands to touch mine. Her energy was powerfully positive and contagious. Without a word, we both understood that in dancing together we would maintain our independence, yet share the experience. When we moved onto the dance floor together, everyone in the place turned to watch Taco Jody and the "old hippie chick." What a sweet communion it was to dance with her.

A month or so later, I said to Inga, "I would like to be your friend. Would you join me for dinner tomorrow?"

"That would be most enjoyable," she said in her quiet, self-assured way. "Thank you, Jody."

At dinner, Inga was charming, gracious, and full of fun, and I learned that she was a renowned author of children's books! She spent a month every summer in Frankfurt, Germany, lecturing and teaching creative writing to children. We discovered that we were born in the same month of the same year — I was eight days older than she — both of us Aries. She had divorced her husband when she was quite young to devote herself to her artistic pursuits, and had no regrets about the decision to follow her passion. She brought her camera to dinner, and the photos of that evening are among my prized possessions. Her note that accompanied them refers to "the celebrated evening we shared."

Shortly after our celebrated evening, Inga left the island never to return. The following winter, I asked her island neighbor about her and was told that Inga had been diagnosed with inoperable cancer, had sold her cottage, and returned to Frankfurt to live out her days in the company of relatives. Though our connection was brief, Inga was enormously important to me. With every passing year I realize more and more what a crucial role model she was: calm, gracious, and absolutely true to herself.

I so much want to encourage others to seek release from the emotional shackles that keep us from realizing our potential as loving and creative human beings. It is my prayer that my story will inspire others — even just one other person — to begin the

Jody Today

journey of self-realization. As we empty ourselves of the negative programming from our past, we become more and more capable of bearing loving witness for others on the path.

And so, having left behind my false self, I keep falling in love with the real me. I may not be able to dance with the same athleticism of my younger years, but *now* when I dance, my movements are imbued with the power and grace of all I have experienced. What a marvelous journey this life continues to be!